THE 15 SUCCESS PRINCIPLES FOR PRINCIPLES FOR SELF-REALIZATION

ALSO BY SARA LANDON

The Wisdom of The Council

The Dream, the Journey, Eternity, and God,
with Mike Dooley

You Are a Channel

All of the above are available at your local bookstore,
or may be ordered by visiting:

Hay House UK: www.hayhouse.co.uk
Hay House USA: www.hayhouse.com®
Hay House Australia: www.hayhouse.com.au
Hay House India: www.hayhouse.co.in

***

THE 15 SUCCESS PRINCIPLES FOR SELF-REALIZATION

———✳———

CHANNELLED WISDOM TO CREATE YOUR REALITY AND EXPAND YOUR PERSPECTIVE

SARA LANDON

HAY HOUSE

Carlsbad, California • New York City
London • Sydney • New Delhi

Published in the United Kingdom by:
Hay House UK Ltd, 1st Floor, Crawford Corner,
91–93 Baker Street, London W1U 6QQ
Tel: +44 (0)20 3927 7290; www.hayhouse.co.uk

Cover design: Mary Anne Smith • Interior design: Bryn Best

A catalogue record for this book is available from the British Library.

Tradepaper ISBN: 978-1-83782-448-9
E-book ISBN: 978-1-4019-9388-7
Audiobook ISBN: 978-1-4019-9389-4

10 9 8 7 6 5 4 3 2 1

This product uses responsibly sourced papers, including recycled materials and materials from other controlled sources. For more information, see www.hayhouse.co.uk

The authorized representative in the EU for product safety and compliance is Penguin Random House Ireland, Morrison Chambers, 32 Nassau Street, Dublin D02 YH68, Ireland. https://eu-contact.penguin.ie

Printed and bound by CPI Group (UK) Ltd, Croydon CR0 4YY

MIX
Paper | Supporting
responsible forestry
FSC
www.fsc.org   FSC® C018179

"Come home to the truth within you,
to the power within you, to the love within you,
to the Source within you, the master that you are,
and remember why you are here.

"You are here of your own choosing,
to be part of the greatest awakening that has
ever occurred in our human experience, to be part
of the greatest potential for a transformation of
human consciousness that has ever
occurred in any lifetime."

— THE COUNCIL

CONTENTS

INTRODUCTION

Hello, and welcome! I am so happy you are here. It's my great joy to support and guide you to live and apply The Council's profound and life-changing wisdom so that you can truly create *your best life*. This is an invitation into self-realization and an opportunity to experience the pure potential and infinite possibilities that exist for you as the powerful Creator of your reality.

I never desired to be a channel, but now I can't imagine my life any other way. For years, I had undeniable experiences: connecting with my deceased brother, receiving messages from the Universe in the form of symbols and angel numbers, and even anticipating what people were going to say or do. Until one day, at the height of my professional career, I had a Quantum Healing Hypnosis Technique session. It changed my life.

In these sessions, my entire body was flooded with energy and warm, liquid love. It was like nothing I had ever felt. It was like being shocked with volts of love, bliss, and ecstasy. I began to speak in these sessions in a voice that was not my own. In the first session, the peculiar voice coming through me went on speaking for over an hour. I was aware of myself but also aware that it wasn't *me* talking. I didn't remember what was said, but I could feel the truth and love in the words that were coming through.

Over time we began to call the voice The Council, as it seemed to be a group of wise old souls providing answers to our many questions, thereby expanding our awareness. We continued with weekly sessions. Each time, more of my consciousness was present to the conversation. Eventually, I was fully aware of the information that was coming through me from The Council. Their messages felt like the deepest truth I had ever known, and as if I were remembering something I already knew.

I began meditating daily, and within minutes I could feel The Council's love and my consciousness merging with theirs. However, I want to emphasize that I never experience The Council as outside of me or as if they are taking me over. My connection with The Council occurs because I connect to a frequency *within me* that allows me to expand my awareness into higher levels of consciousness, which have always been there and available to me.

The wisdom of The Council has now expanded into courses, books, seminars, summits, retreats, and a global community of people living The Council's wisdom and teachings. And *I live a life beyond my wildest dreams,* just as they assured me I would. Since channeling and integrating The Council's wisdom, my life has more love, joy, abundance, freedom, well-being, and harmony than I ever thought possible.

There is more information in the world now than ever before, with the Internet, social media, and so many great teachers, books, and courses available. However, all the wisdom in the world will not create the life of your dreams . . . if you don't live it and apply it in your life! In this book, you will receive the channeled wisdom that will expand your perspective and show you exactly *how* you create your reality, and the process, tools, and real-life examples of how to live and apply these success principles.

The wisdom and vibrational frequency contained within this book are your guideposts to implementing the foundational success principles for self-realization. Self-realization is *why you are here,* the very reason that you have chosen *this life* experience during the greatest awakening of human consciousness that has ever occurred in any lifetime. Your highest potential is to fully awaken to the truth of who you are and then allow your own natural evolution into self-realization. Once you have experienced self-realization, all that is asked of you is to live fully, love fully, and be all that you are.

What is self-realization? The Council defines it as the integration of every part of you, the part of you that is Source, God, the Divine, the part of you that is soul, spirit, higher self, the part of you that is this magnificent, beautiful human with a unique, celebrated personality and characteristics expressed only through you. It's also that innocent little girl or little boy within you—the inner child part of you. And it's every part of you along the way. It is what you have experienced thus far—in this lifetime and every lifetime—and it is who you are becoming, even though you are everything you wish to be; you already are. To self-realize is to not deny any part of yourself. It is fully allowing every part of yourself to align with your wholeness, completeness, and divine perfection.

It is important to embrace, be compassionate and loving to every part of you, and not to fight against or reject any part of you. To fight against the idea of an ego is to deny and war against some unworthy or unwanted part of yourself. Self-realization is an experience of wholeness, to fully invite in the part of you that is soul and spirit, the part of you that has the grandest perspective of all that you are and all that's going on here, and the part of you that is the energy and the consciousness that creates everything. It might also be referred to as the fulfillment of your purpose or your highest potential.

Some of my students describe it best. One student explains self-realization like this: "For the first time ever I am having the experience that *absolutely nothing could make me any happier than I am right now.*" Another student describes it as "It's the whole Universe in this moment supporting me and my knowing that I truly am one with All That Is." The next student described it as "Unable to define with words—it's just so glorious." Another explanation one student had: "Self-realization is *pure bliss.* The first time in my life I experienced myself beyond fear and the feeling that I wasn't good enough."

To evolve is to become self-realized. It's a natural process, and you will get there through allowing. Don't entangle with your own self-judgment or comparison. Don't create resistance and try to force it. There's no expectation. Love yourself exactly where you are. Don't compare your journey to anyone else's. Whenever you allow yourself into the experience of self-realization is absolutely perfect. My intention is that this book and the wisdom within will help you to experience self-realization consciously and intentionally, and to be aware that it's available to you in every moment.

Self-realization connects you to the consciousness and the energy that is Source, God, the Divine. It is the realization that you *are* that consciousness and energy. It's not about performing miracles like walking on water or turning lead to gold. However, you might notice miracles happening in your life on a daily basis. It's not about becoming superhuman or doing supernatural things like reading someone's mind or becoming psychic, though it can connect you more deeply to your mastery, inherent gifts, and latent abilities. It is about *energy*. The energy is yours and here to serve you in your abundance, well-being, freedom, joy, and love.

Self-realization is the feeling of pure bliss, pure love, peace, pure Oneness with everything. It is the state of consciousness where all your power is available to you. It is where your gifts of intuition are uncovered and activated. It is a place where you can live in your heart fully as the pure love that you are. It's not about doing anything; it's about being all that you are.

Here are a few key points that might be helpful as you begin. When I first heard the term *allowing*, I found it incredibly annoying and frustrating. I constantly questioned: How *does* one allow? What does it even *mean* to allow? And how could it possibly be *that* important? Allow, allow, allow. However, I will tell you, it is quite possibly *the* most important thing you can do.

I will make it simple for you. The instant manifestation of allowing is *joy*. To get into a state of allowing, begin to focus on joy, and think of what brings you joy. Focus on thoughts that are joyful, remember joyful memories, and begin to intentionally do the things that bring you joy. Ask yourself the question, "What brings me joy?" If you are in a state of joy, you are allowing.

One final note: as you read, you will notice The Council will refer to you as a *master*. If you drew this book to you, you are, indeed, a master. As a master, you possess the wisdom you have acquired throughout all your incarnations in physical form and throughout your soul's entire journey. It is not intended to mean that you are a master *over* any other or imply that hierarchically you are better than any other. Being a *master* in human form simply means living as a *realized* being: You *realize* yourself as more than just human; you *realize* yourself as *All That Is*, as Source, as God, as Light, as the Divine, and you *realize* the dream in your heart for Heaven on Earth—for peace, for joy, for love, for harmony, for well-being, for abundance, for beauty and freedom for all.

My own desire to discover my truth, my purpose, and the meaning of life is what summoned the consciousness of The Council. If you are reading this now, I can say the same for you. You drew this book to you at just the perfect time. You, too, are a channel of Divine Love and higher wisdom—a part of The Council on Earth.

I've dedicated countless hours to channeling The Council's wisdom and sharing their messages to all who are ready to receive them. These are my deepest, heartfelt wishes for you:

> *May you remember the infinite wisdom that lies within you.*
> *May you reconnect with the light that you are.*
> *May you realize yourself as a powerful extension of Source Energy.*

I have devoted my life to living The Council's profound, life-changing wisdom each and every day. I welcome you to join me on this incredible journey of self-realization. This book is potentially my greatest gift to the world, and creating it for you has been the joy of a lifetime.

Realization is not something that your human mind can do or figure out or make happen. It is your natural state of being—and your natural evolution. You allow your realization to occur through the integration of all that you are!

This is the opportunity of a lifetime to, once and for all, *answer the call* to remember who you really are, why you are here, and *all* that you intended when you chose this magnificent life experience. Are you ready to accept your invitation and allow your own self-realization? Let's begin!

The Council's Foundational Teachings

Before we begin, I'd like to share The Council's core teachings to give you a strong knowledge base of where they are coming from when they deliver their messages to you.

The wisdom of The Council and its impact is multifaceted. Their unique perspective, their sometimes unusual way of saying things, and their obvious love for us affects us in many ways. Those of us compelled by their wisdom, however, find the *truths* they bring forward to be the most impactful when used as a guide to self-realization. These truths include:

- You are everything you wish to be, you already are.

- You are the Creator within your own creation of reality.

- Life is meant to be joyful.

- What you focus on and the meaning you give it is what creates your reality.

- Consciousness moves energy into form; this is the formula for all creation.

- There is only love.

- Everything is always happening *for* you, not *to* you.

- You are Source Energy that *you* focused into a physical body.

- If you want to experience anything in the world around you, you must first create it within yourself.

- You have everything you need within you—and an infinite supply of resources—to create the life of your dreams.

- You have come here by your own choosing from an expanded state of consciousness to experience life (energy) in physical form.

- Life is a grand adventure, and the journey only continues on from here.

- All your power is in the now moment.

- Stillness is the access point to acceleration.

- There is no need to make big decisions about anything; allow all things to be *choiceless*.

- As you align to a higher level of consciousness, your well-being and abundance are assured.

- True Creation has no agenda.

- You get more of what you *are*, not what you *want*. If you want more joy in your life, align to the joy that is already within you and around you.

- When you are resisting anything, you are resisting everything and stopping the flow of easy, effortless, harmonious creation.

An Invitation to Self-Realization from The Council

We are so very pleased and delighted to be here with you on this fine day. We tell you that while our words to you are important, this is a vibrational experience of you remembering the truth of who you are and why you are here and *all* that you intended when you chose this magnificent life experience.

You are coming into the time of *realization*—the full realization of all that you are. Everything is here for you. The energy is here for you. The wisdom is here for you. The consciousness is here for you. The vibration is here for you. It is all here. It is all available to you now. It is of your choosing. Choosing to recognize your moments of realization will just deepen and strengthen and expand your moments of realization, fully integrating all that you are, choosing for you, stepping into higher levels of consciousness, and *living there.*

You are indeed a realized master having a human experience. You came from consciousness. You focused yourself into this human experience. You chose for this to be the lifetime that you would fully step into realization, enlightenment, and then ascension into living in higher levels of consciousness while still being in physical form, but you never meant to *exclude* formless creation, and you never meant to get so attached and specific about creation that was *in* physical form.

It is all here for you. If you were going to get attached to any physical form, get attached and excited and delighted and totally savor all that is here for you *now.* The sun, the moon, the stars, the planet, the land, the animals, each other. You are all here for each other, and it is all here for you. There is nothing going on anywhere *out there* that is better than you living here as a truly realized, enlightened master ascending to the highest levels of consciousness that are available to you here on Earth now.

What are you waiting for? *What are you waiting for?* Whose permission do you need? Whose forgiveness do you need? Whose attention do you need? No one's. You are the only one who can set yourself free to be all that you are, to live your life fully, to love yourself fully, and to choose the experiences you want to have for you.

You are here to live your life fully. When you ask, "What is my purpose?", "Why am I here?", "What am I supposed to do?", or "What should I do?"; we'll tell you *live your life to the fullest.* Oh, love yourself fully. Be all that you are and choose the experiences you want to have for you.

We will break each one of these down more specifically. Number one: Live. Live. *Live.* Don't wait. Don't delay. Live. You're not waiting for anything to happen. You're not waiting for anyone to happen. You're not waiting for anything. You're not waiting for any amount of money. Live. You're not waiting for permission. *Live. Live your life fully.*

What does that mean for you? If it comes up that you *can't*, then that is the choice you are making. If you say, "I'd love to. I'd love to live my life fully, but I *can't* because my body won't, because my finances won't, because he won't let me, because she won't let me," that is a choice you are making. That is power that you are giving to something outside of you.

Your power is for you and only you. Only you can choose for you, and only you can set yourself free, and only *you* can choose to live the life that you want to live for you. No apologies. No exceptions. No delays. No excuses. No putting the responsibility of you living your life fully in the hands of anyone outside of you.

All of your power is for you. Choose it. Live your life fully each day. Allow your life to be everything you intended it to be—exciting, fulfilling, passionate, alive, creative. Dance and play with all of creation. Live your life fully. Full. Satiated. Filled up. Savoring every moment. Live your life fully. You do not need anyone's permission. It doesn't matter what's going on *out there.* It matters what's going on *right here and now.*

Others may not understand. Others may not agree. Others may not approve. Are you going to give them that power over you and your life? As long as you know this one thing, as long as you know this *one thing,* then there is nothing you cannot do. Then there is nothing that you cannot navigate with ease and grace, then there is nothing ever going on that is not happening *for* you and serving in your highest enlightenment when you know that you can always come back to presence, consciousness, and awareness in *this* moment and *every* moment, no matter what is going on out there. Accept and know that you are choosing realization.

You are choosing realization when no matter what is going on out there, no matter what they say, no matter what you're seeing in the world around you, that *you can come into the moment here and now.* Breathe, move from your head down into your being, into your body, into your power source. You can expand this moment. You can put some space around yourself, and you can fill that space with light. You can expand this moment as far as you can see in every direction where there is no place that you are not because you are so focused, all of your power in the now moment, conscious, aware, present, aligned, here and now, no matter what is going on out there. Then you know that you can always choose realization in any moment, which means you can live your life fully without fear, without fear of rejection, without fear of disapproval, without fear of failure.

When you live your life fully, and you let energy and light guide the way for you, and you get good at being so present in the moment that you are just in the flow and it's like *life is moving you with perfect ease and alignment and harmony in every moment,* oh, it's so good. It's so good. Live your life fully. It's here for you now more so than ever before. This is a great opportunity. This time is a great gift to you.

You have multiple potentials and possibilities available to you in every moment: life fulfilment, love fulfilment, joy fulfilment, adventure fulfilment, excitement fulfilment, and creativity fulfilment on every level. We are here to expand your consciousness. We are here to expand your awareness of what is possible for you so that you can begin to perceive your life from the highest levels, so that you can begin to draw to you all sorts of realities that are expanded, fulfilling, exciting, passionate.

Living fully—that is why you're here. Live with no regrets, no doubts, no second guessing yourself, no needing anyone's approval or agreement for you to live *your* life to the fullest. Not just this life that you know as you, but all the different potentials and possibilities that are available to you. You can live a life as a person in the mountains, in a cabin with a log fire and a garden, and one with animals. You can live a life in a city with adventure and music and culture and art. You can live a life with that person, and you can have an experience with this person. You can explore all the different potentials and possibilities because you never meant to limit your experience to just the creations that are expressed in physical form. You never meant to diminish the limitless, formless creations that all add to your ability to live fully.

Anything and everything is possible for you. When you start allowing yourself to live fully in *every* potential and possibility that is available to you, oh, you're going to live in ways that very few have ever experienced. But because you have, you pave the way, you guide the way, you blaze the trail to what it's like to live your life fully. And then many others who are ready will also allow themselves to live fully.

That's really what you want. *To be totally satiated here and now because you realized all that is here and now.*

What is realization? The integration of every part of you. What is realization? Realizing everything that is here for you now, in form, in formless, potentials, possibilities, but also being totally satiated and savoring *all* that is here for you.

You could not in one lifetime savor all the beautiful places on your planet, all the incredible, magnificent, beautiful things in nature. You couldn't imagine all the different animals and the plant kingdom and all the things that are here for you. You couldn't even love all the people who you *really* love. There's no end to the potentials and the possibilities of people to love, of things to love, of people to enjoy, of things to enjoy, of beauty in nature, and beauty in the land, and beauty in people, and beauty in places, beauty in ideas, beauty in visions, beauty in books and songs and music. You couldn't even take it all in if you tried. But just *try.*

What if *that* was your life's purpose? There is an unlimited amount, a limitless, unquantifiable, unmeasurable, uncontainable amount of beauty on this planet in this life, in this human experience, *for you.*

Just try. Just *choose* that you're going to experience as much as you possibly can. Choose it.

But what keeps you from it? What keeps you from living fully? One thing. *Your own love of self.* Your own self-love. Your own worthiness. Your own knowing of who you really are and why you are here and all that you intended.

Who do you love the most? Choose the answer to be *you*, because when you really love you, oh, then you can really love others. When you really celebrate who you are, then you can really celebrate others. When you really appreciate who you are, then you can really appreciate others. The more you enjoy the good in you, the more you can enjoy the good in others. The more you see your own *infinite* worth, the more you feel your own infinite worth; the more you experience your own infinite worth, the more you can see it and feel it and experience it in others.

Self-love, love of self. In those moments that you really, really love yourself and all of who you are, and you *allow* all of who you are, you really allow every part of you because there is no right or wrong. You have had all sorts of different experiences based on different levels of consciousness you were in; and all led to data and information that served your highest realization, enlightenment, expansion, clarity, and creativity. All of it served you in every way. So, receive it and embrace it.

You'll know you're really experiencing realization when giving and receiving become one, when you see that giving is receiving and receiving is giving, and you never deny it for yourself. You never stop giving and you never stop receiving, because you are a force field of creation. You are consciousness. You are a force field. There's no end to you, there's no beginning to you. There's an expansion of you, there's a contraction of you.

Expansion of *you* feels so good. Your heart is filled with love. You're beaming with light. You're radiant. You're magnificent. You're inspired. You're passionate. You're creative. You're open and expanding and allowing. It's all in you, this force field that is you. Within this force field that is you is consciousness because that is what you *are*. When you're in this expansive force field of consciousness and this consciousness fills this entire force field, then consciousness is what moves energy into form, into life.

Consciousness is what moves light into life. You are a force field of consciousness, and the more expanded you are, the *more* energy that is experienced or felt or in your force field. Then particles of infinite creation respond to the consciousness, respond to the energy, and you begin to know yourself for all that you are. You start *expressing* all that you are, and you live in the freedom of *being* all that you are.

Love yourself fully. Love yourself. Take the time you need for you. Have boundaries. Say what is okay for you. Care for yourself. Have a relationship with yourself. Love yourself first and foremost, and you will experience love like you've never experienced love in physical form yet.

You think you love your children now; you think you love your grandchildren now; you think you love your lovers and your partners and your spouses and your friends now; but *wait until you really allow yourself to love yourself and come into the realization of your own love of self.* Same people, even more love. Your capacity to love expands beyond anything you've felt before.

Many of you ask about connections to your higher self, connections to Source, connections to collectives and higher dimensional beings and connections into higher levels of consciousness. It's a relationship no different than any other relationship you have. If you doubt it, if you don't trust it, if you don't make time for it, if you only go there when things are wrong and you're complaining, you're not going to experience the relationship with Source that is possible for you.

Imagine what kind of a relationship you would have with someone if they always doubted you. They didn't trust you. They never trusted you. They're always doubting you. They never make time for you. They're never available to you, and the only time they come to you is when they have a problem that they want you to fix, when they need something and they want you to give it to them.

Now imagine if you treated someone else like that. You're always doubting them, you cannot trust them, you never really spend much time with them, you only connect when there's a problem. This is what so many of you do in your connection to the Source that is you, the Source that is you that creates worlds, the Source that is you that is always one with infinite intelligence, the Source that is you that is always one with infinite well-being, the Source that is you that is always one with infinite abundance, the Source that is you that is always one with infinite love of everything and everyone eternally.

There is no greater relationship. There is no more important relationship. All other relationships will just be a mere reflection of your own relationship to Source, the Source that is you, the Source, the consciousness, the energy, the force field, the Creator within your own creation that is you. You might say that any relationship that you have that is *really good* is that way because there is so much love. Your relationship with Source reflects your own love of Self.

Love yourself. Be all that you are. When that is the most important thing to you, then all else will reflect back your importance, your brilliance, your magnificence, your love, your potential, your divinity.

Choose the experiences that you want to have for you. Not by forcing energy. Not by trying to control it. Many of you have come to this place where you believe that your relationship with Source is a passive one, that you're sitting here waiting, passively waiting for the Universe to divinely orchestrate something for you and *then* you will really start living your life. But you think you are waiting. You're not waiting. *You're always choosing.*

Choose the experiences that you want to have for you. Choose, choose, choose. You're Creator within your own creation. Creators choose what they wish to create; however, as we have said, without an agenda, without force, without effort and struggle and sacrifice. Choose. True Creation has no personal agenda.

True Creation has no personal agenda. Not trying to attract that certain amount of money. Not trying to get that certain job. Not that certain person. Not that certain thing. Doesn't have to be so certain. Doesn't have to be so specific. But that doesn't mean you don't choose.

You can choose to have more connection. You can choose to have more love. You can choose to have more abundance. You can choose to have more *coming from your wholeness*, knowing that you get more of what you are. Choose more beauty. Choose more abundance. Choose more love.

Now, yes, you can decide that you really want to create greater health and well-being. You can choose that. Then you can let the energy and the light guide the way because it is your focus, it is your perception, it is what you're giving your attention to that is aligning those particles of infinite creation for you. Infinite.

Those particles of infinite creation are responding to you. They're responding to what you're focused on. They're responding to what you're aligning to. They're responding to how you're perceiving. They're responding to what you're giving your attention to. So, choose. But if you're saying, "I can't," that is also a choice. If you're saying, "She won't let me"—or "He won't let you"—then that's also a choice. If you're saying, "I can't because of the money," that's also a choice. If you're saying, "I can't because of this body," then that's also a choice.

You still don't really know how powerful you are, but you're *starting* to get it. You're starting to understand the limitless, powerful Creator that you are. The most important choice you make, especially right now, is to decide, to choose that you're there, that you've got it, that you *are* realized, that you *are* enlightened, that you *are* ascended, that you *are* a master, that you *are* an ascended master here on Earth, and then choose to *live like one*.

Right here, right now, this is the life in which you have *chosen* to fully step into realization and know yourself as the true realized master that you are. Everything that has happened until now has been preparing you for this time, for the here and now. Everything has prepared you, everything has been preparing you, everything has been happening for you. Know without any doubt, *know* that everything is serving in your realization and enlightenment.

If an incredible lover has come into your life, assume and *know* that they are here as part of your realization. If you have an amount of money that has come into your life, *know* that that has come in for your realization. If suddenly, your body is feeling so good and rested and alive, then *know* that that's happening for your realization. All other examples are also true. Everything that's happening on your planet right now is happening for *your* realization—*for you*.

Can you take that in? Can you accept that it's all for you? Yes, many others will come into realization at this time, but it doesn't mean that it's not *all here for you.*

To come into realization is to realize that you are realized. You might find yourself saying, "I just had a realization. I just had a moment of enlightenment. I just realized. I just got it. I got it. *I get it.* I'm home. *I'm home.* I'm here. It's now."

You're here. You're realized. The struggle is over. The search is over. The seeking is over. You're here. You're home. It's now. Choose to feel it in every cell of your body. Choose to align every cell of your body. Choose to direct every particle of infinite creation in the force field of consciousness that is you. Align it to the here-and-now realized moment because there's nothing better anywhere but here and now in this full realization of all that you are, of all that you are.

What the world needs most from you is for you to allow this realization of all that you are, to know yourself as the realized master that you are, and then to live like one, to live fully, to love fully, to be all that you are. Then you step into ascension, expansion, consciousness at the highest levels.

There's so much here, and it is so much fun. You will know what it is really like to play and create in new levels of ascended master consciousness. You will serve, and you will contribute. You will raise the vibration of the planet, and you will raise the consciousness of the planet. You will serve and contribute in ways that you could never understand, but *you will not doubt it because you will be having so much fun playing, creating, loving, oh, living.*

That is what the world needs most from you, *however* that feels good to you, *however* you choose for you. *But choose for you.* You're not waiting. It's here now. You don't need anyone's permission. You gave yourself the permission you need. You don't need anyone else's approval because you finally have chosen to allow all that you are, to be all that you are, and to integrate every part of you, every part of you.

True Creation, true mastery, aligned to the I Am Creator frequency, is mastering impeccable creative expression that is dedicated to the highest good, the highest evolution of all. You're going to see so clearly how much of your life was based in motivation that came from fear, that came from lack, that came from limitation. And you're going to see with eyes of love and innocence and absolute forgiveness, you're going to see how you held *yourself* in limitation, how you held *yourself* in lack, how your need to control made you feel so out of control, why your feeling like a victim just created more experiences of it. You're going to see where your emotions manifested in your body as a direct reflection of what was going on in your emotional layer because your body, the magnificent machine that it is, was communicating with you about what was in your highest good.

See it for all that it is. See it for its *perfection*. *Everything* is responding to you. *Everything* is a reflection of you and your relationship with Source and with you. There is no *out there*. Everything is a figment of your own creation.

There is nothing out there. It's all reflecting to you your relationship with you, how you are relating to you. Because your attention and focus and all of your choosing is out there, none of your power is here for you. They're choosing for you, they're deciding for you. You're focused on them and what they want you to do, and on what they say you can and can't do. So, the reflection of not having your power is how you are relating. It's a reflection of you.

You take *all that power* back into this moment, and you move into your consciousness and your awareness here and now, and you expand the force field that you are, you expand the consciousness that you are, and you sit here, Creator within your own creation, the center of *your* universe, and you powerfully focus and direct and choose for you. *That* is mastering impeccable creative expression dedicated to the highest evolution of all—of all that you are, all that is possible for you, all the potentials that are available to you.

Live your life fully. That is why you are here. Live it. Live it and love it. This is what it's all about.

You are birthing something. You're birthing someone new, the *new you*, the you who lives in higher levels of consciousness and awareness, the you who is now playing and creating in new levels of consciousness. You are birthing the new you. The greatest thing that you could do is not take *any* of the old parts of who you thought you were, to wake up fresh and renewed every day like a beautiful brand-new day.

How do you want to live *today*? What do you want to experience *today*? What would bring you the greatest joy *today*? What would totally satiate you *today*? Who do you want to be *today*? What potential and possibility and timeline do you want to explore *today*? New you, new day. Every day, clean slate. If you approached your life in that way, oh, you would understand True Creation, you would understand the I Am Creator frequency and the power that it has, and, most importantly, you would understand yourself as Creator within your own creation.

Realize that you are realized. Realize that you are now realized and notice it as often as possible throughout the day. *I get it. I just had a realization. I just felt realization. I just felt enlightenment. I just felt Oneness. I just felt God. I just felt myself as the God that I am, the Source that I am, the master that I am. I just felt what it's like to be living mastery. I just felt my ascended master self.*

Realize it. Feel it. Bring it all into this force field that is you, every particle of infinite creation responding to you as the realized master that you *are*. And so it is.

Remember, the one thing that will support you in transcending fear, support you in transcending chaos and doubt and worry, is when you *know* you can *always* come back into the present moment, into your consciousness, into awareness, that you can elevate your consciousness and awareness, that you can come fully into the now moment. You can put some space around yourself, you can breathe, you can feel into the force field that you are, you can expand this force field. You can open to all that you are because you know that everything is always serving you, is serving in your enlightenment, is serving in your realization, is serving in your ascension, is serving you in the highest and best good always.

Everything is serving you. Know it. Feel it. Feel it in this moment. Feel it in your consciousness. Feel it in your body. Feel it in your being. Feel it in the force field of creation that you are. That is to know what ascension feels like. Having transcended fear, worry, struggle, chaos, suffering forevermore. And so it is.

You are stepping into paradise. You are choosing it with your power, with your freedom, with your love, for the experience of paradise here on Earth. You're here to create *your* Heaven on Earth. You have the power to do so. You are free to do so. You do so through focusing the Divine Love that you are on what it is you want *more* of in your paradise—your creation of Heaven on Earth.

This is an expansion of the realization that you have been coming into alignment with for some time. You are expanding that realization; not only into the realization of the power within you, not only the realization of the master that you are, not only the integration of every part of you, but the integration of everything that is *here* for you. You're coming into the realization and the integration of all that is here for you. You come to the realization of all that you are so that you can live freely and love fully and be who you really are.

Realization is the integration of every part of you, no longer denying any part of your magnificent personality or your experiences. They all provided data and information that led you to this place now, and *it's perfect*. You are coming into realization instead of separating yourself and moving into lower dimensions of consciousness, which entangle you with lack, limitation, fear, and separation. It is the realization of every part of you and the integration of every part of you, the Source Energy part of you, the master part of you, the ascended master part of you, the human part of you, the multidimensional nature part of you, the aspects of you in every dimension that are awakening and coming into the realization of all that you are from the highest awareness of your being as multidimensional.

You don't need to intellectualize it. You don't need to understand it, but you *are* fully coming into the realization and integration of every part of you. And then you're expanding into the realization of all that is here for you—the resources, connections, opportunities, synchronicity, Divine orchestration, the love, the peace, the joy, the harmony, the abundance, the well-being, the aspects of nature and the animal kingdom—all here for you. It is the experience of your complete and total integration of the perfection of all that you are into the divinely woven tapestry of humanity.

You're coming into the realization of the perfection of this experience. You're coming into the perfection and realization of all that is here for you—infinite abundance, infinite love, infinite well-being, infinite intelligence. No end to anything ever. No separation from anything. Indeed, the abundance of Heaven on Earth is here for you now. The abundance of the Promised Land. There is a *knowing*. It has been prophesized. It has been known somewhere inside of you that you *would* come into the realization of the Promised Land, promised before you focused yourself into this incarnation. You promised it to you—promised, guaranteed, assured, it could be no other way. And so it is.

PART I

EXPANDING
YOUR PERSPECTIVE

*"It is through the light, your light, that you see the
grander perspective here in all things, in all situations,
in all circumstances. It is through the light, your light, that you hold
the vision for all beings living in peace and joy and harmony and
abundance for all. It is through the light, your light, that humanity
will realize, through the energy that is coming forth, through the
light that is shining bright, that there is a potential and a possibility
that exists here and now for peace and joy and harmony and love
and freedom and abundance for all. It is through the light, through
your light, that all of this not only becomes possible, not only a
potential, but a realization for yourself and those around you, a
realization, a dream within your heart that becomes a dream
within a masterpiece, that becomes a masterpiece painted and
expressed as reality, molded, created, painted, realized."*

— THE COUNCIL

In Part One, we will focus on the Success Principles for Expanding Your Perspective. The wisdom of The Council is here to help you remember who you are, why you're here, what your purpose is, and how to live it. Ultimately, The Council's wisdom is intended to expand your perspective on who you really are and what is possible for you. Your life is meant to be magnificent. *You are magnificent.* Your life is meant to be a grand adventure.

You are here in this incredible life experience for expansion, for expression, and for experiences. You are here for the very expansion of your own consciousness, of human consciousness, and the expansion of possibilities and potentials within the human experience. You are expanding your own consciousness, expanding your own potentials and possibilities, and therefore contributing to the expansion of all potentials and possibilities within the human experience just by you living an extraordinary, magical, miraculous life.

You are here for expansion. Feel into expansion. Oh, it is vast and glorious indeed. Feel into the place where anything and everything is possible for you. Feel into expansion, the place where all is known. Feel into expansion, where everything you want and need comes to you. Feel into expansion, where you are connected to everything and everyone.

Expand consciously and intentionally. Allow all that you have expanded into. Imagine you in this moment, expanding deep into the Earth beneath you, from the bottom of your feet, into the roots of the trees, into the ground beneath you, into the crust of the Earth, all the way down, all the way down into the center of the Earth.

Expand beneath you as far as you can perceive. Expand all around you from this moment. Expand, fill up the room that you're in, the home that you're in, the town that you're in, the state that you're in, the country that you're in, the continent that you're on. Expand over the oceans, across the entire globe. Expand. Expand. Expand.

Expand from the crown of your head up to the tops of the trees, up to the clouds in the sky, up to the moon and the stars and the sun. Expand as far as you can perceive above you, beneath you, in every direction around you. Expand. Expand. Expand.

Feel the vast and glorious expansion of your consciousness, of the force field of consciousness that you are. Expand such that every particle of infinite creation is within you, responding to you, one with you, such that everything and anything is possible for you, such that every possibility and potential is within you, available to you.

Expand into every corner of this Universe, where there is no separation. All is known. All is you. All is within you. All is available to you. Expand into all that you are, all that you will ever be, all that you have become. Expand. Expand. Expand.

Bring all of your expansion back into this present moment, here and now. Bring it all back into this present moment, here and now. Feel into your expansion and remember the power of this present moment, here and now.

If you are worried about anything, if you are struggling with anything, if you are anxious, if you are in resistance, you are not in the now, here moment. You can solve any challenge, any issue, anything that's worrying you or bothering you by simply coming back into the now, here moment, into the now moment, into your power, into your presence, into an awareness and a consciousness of this now, here moment while also feeling into the expansion of all that you are and all that you will ever be, without any need to figure it out, force anything, without any worry or stress or anxiety.

All of your power is in the now moment. And the magical, miraculous part of life is allowing the next perfect step to come to you by being in your power in the moment, allowing the next perfect step to come to you, allowing the next perfect, logical step to present itself to you because you are in the now moment while also aligned to all that you have expanded into and all that you are.

You aren't meant to figure it out. You aren't meant to push and force and effort. You aren't meant to struggle and suffer. You are not meant to live in a state of resistance. You are meant to live in the present.

This now moment is all there is. When you get to the next moment, it will only and ever be that now moment. And anything that's ever happened only and ever happened in that now moment. All that exists is the now moment. All of your power is in the now moment.

When you are in your power, in the now moment, expanding the force field of consciousness that is you, such that every particle of infinite creation in all the Universe is within you and responding to you, we assure you in all situations the logical, obvious, next perfect step will come to you. It will appear under your feet as you follow the energy and let the light guide the way. The next perfect step will be logical and obvious, and it will come to you. The more you allow the expansion that is here for you now, that you have been elevating yourself into, the more you will see magical and miraculous potentials and possibilities present themselves to you in the moment here and now.

You are everything you wish to be.
You already are.

"You are everything you wish to be. You already are. It is all within you. It always has been. It always will be. And so it is."

— THE COUNCIL

Many years ago, before I even knew who The Council was and began channeling them, I was doing automatic writing. Almost every time I tuned in to do automatic writing, the same statement came to me: "You are everything you wish to be, you already are." I could feel the truth of this statement in every cell of my body, although I could not explain *how* I knew that it was true. Yet, I had spent my life trying to accomplish things, trying to achieve things, trying to do more to *be enough*, trying to earn my way to worthiness. You might be able to relate with the same feeling . . .

From a young age, you are often told what things you are supposed to do, what things you should do, what things you are not supposed to do, what things would please those around you. Most people spend most of their lives identifying themselves with all the things outside of them that aren't really who they are. The Council says, "Nothing that ever happens in this human experience can ever threaten your infinite worth, and there is nothing that you can ever do or achieve in this human experience that could make you any more worthy." *You are everything you wish to be, you already are.* You are connected to All That Is, which means that you are the Source Energy and the consciousness that has created *everything*.

Sometimes The Council says, "You're everything you wish to be, you already are. It is all within you, it always will be," and sometimes they say, "It's all within you and it always has been." You have everything you need within you and an infinite supply of resources available to you to create the life of your dreams. It's not the creating of the life of your dreams that makes you worthy. It is *knowing* that you are everything you wish to be, you already are, knowing that you have everything within you and an infinite supply of resources available to you to create the life of your dreams, to create your best life, to be the greatest version of you, and live your highest potential in life, whatever that means for you.

The essence of each one of these Success Principles comes back to this foundational teaching that *you are everything you wish to be, you already are, it is all within you, it always will be . . .* The whole Universe, and all of the Source Energy within it, is here for you and available for you to live your highest potential, to create your reality, and explore the magnificent journey to becoming.

This entire planet is here for you. This entire Earth experience and everything it includes is here for you. There is a continuation of everything, there is an expansion of everything, but you are everything you wish to be, you already are.

This is the one and only life that you are focused on now, and this is the time to move fully into every potential, every possibility, open every timeline and begin to play in the infinite possibilities as you summon the energy to create your masterpiece, as you summon the energy to bring Heaven to Earth, as you summon the energy to create paradise on Earth, to embody your highest potential, and expand the potentials and the possibilities for all of humankind.

If you have felt *called* to discover your purpose or felt as if there is some greater calling for your life, it is to awaken to the truth of who you are and then move fully into self-realization. As you do, you expand your awareness of what is *really* possible for you and begin to consciously, intentionally, and confidently create your life and your reality the way you desire it to be.

You are the power that creates worlds, and you are the power that creates *your* world. When you understand this, there is no need to control anything. There's no need to control anyone. There is no fear. There are no feelings of powerlessness. There are no feelings of unworthiness. You experience ultimate freedom: the ultimate freedom in your body, the ultimate freedom in your relationships, the ultimate freedom financially, the ultimate freedom in your expression.

What is the highest potential? What is the ultimate expression? You're here in physical form. You are here to play with energy. You are here to summon energy.

You come from higher vibration. You come from higher frequency. You are summoning higher vibrations and frequencies. You're summoning more energy. Where does that energy come from? Most would say the realm of God, Source Energy, the Divine, Creator. Where does one go when they leave the density of the body? To this place called Heaven, a higher dimension. Heaven on Earth is merely you allowing yourself to summon that energy into physical form, into the Earth, into the physical, into the form.

That's the grand experiment here. That's what's going on. And now you can fully move yourself into the awareness, into the consciousness of having it all, because you are the consciousness and the awareness. You are the consciousness and the energy that creates it all, that has created it all. And there is nothing, dear master, that you cannot create. There's nothing, dear master, that you cannot realize. You are Creator within your own creation of reality. *You are everything you wish to be. You already are.*

This is an awareness beyond anything you've ever allowed yourself to perceive before, which means it must begin to draw to you new experiences beyond anything you've ever experienced in your reality before. It's time for you to create your reality in line with your masterpiece, aligned to your Heaven on Earth, aligned to your vision for paradise on Earth, because it *is* all here for you.

All you need do is summon the energy. You don't have to try to control where it goes. You have the greatest power when you allow yourself to be free and you allow the freedom of energy to flow. You will experience magic and miracles and grand manifestations and moment after moment after moment of true, impeccable, magnificent creation.

Take some deep, intentional, conscious breaths. This is a vibrational experience moving you into an awareness and a level of consciousness beyond any place you've allowed yourself to go. There's nothing to do. Allow the energy. Summon the energy. Feel the energy. Get your entire being into the joy of delighting in all this energy. Activate your physical senses to perceive this energy. You can see it, you can hear it, you can taste it, you can touch it, you can smell it. You're even *thinking* about this energy. That's how clear and powerful and intentional you are.

Bring it all into your body. Bring the activation, bring the coding, bring the frequency all back into you. All you have expanded into is within you now. You are powerful. You are Divine. You are everything you wish to be. You already are. Now simply summon the energy for your magnificent creation of your life and the fulfillment of your highest potential.

YOU ARE A FORCE FIELD OF CONSCIOUSNESS

You are connected to *everything*. Go beyond the illusion of separation into the awareness of pure love, that you are that pure love, and that everything is available to you in a state of pure love.

Begin to expand your perspective to understand that you're not separate, that you really are connected to everything, that you are pure love, and that you are a force field of consciousness. Within that force field of consciousness is infinite abundance, infinite well-being, infinite love, and infinite intelligence. Everything is within you and available to you, including an infinite supply of resources to create the life of your dreams.

You can manifest a lot of things and amass a lot of *stuff*, and still not feel fulfillment, like you are living your purpose, or like you are *good enough*. Once you expand your perspective and begin to embody a state of consciousness where you know that you're already everything you wish to be, life becomes more fun, more playful, more joyful. You align to your wholeness, completeness, and perfection to create with joy and ease. You allow yourself to play, create, and have fun as you choose the experiences that you desire from a knowing that you are worthy of living the life of your dreams with infinite resources that are available to you.

You are always expanding and becoming more. While you are everything you wish to be, you already are, you're always expanding and becoming more. It's a journey. It's a journey of *becoming*. But nothing you do or manifest is going to make you more worthy. You already are infinitely worthy . . .

A helpful practice is to become aware of when you are *denying* what you are worth, when you are denying that you are everything you wish to be. Notice thoughts like, "I'll be more worthy when I do this, I'll be better when I have that, I'll be more lovable when I accomplish this."

If you notice that your mind wants to argue with you about a part of you that isn't good enough, or a part of you that made a mistake, or you think of something you feel guilty about or something you feel ashamed of, accept that you did the *best you could with what you knew at the time.* Now you are expanding your perspective, remembering who you really are, and integrating every part of you into pure love.

You are on a journey through different levels of consciousness that are available to you in the human experience. Some of those dimensions are characterized by separation—separating yourself from Source, separating yourself from others, separating yourself even within yourself, denying that part of you that wasn't smart enough, fast enough, healthy enough, pretty enough, tall enough, thin enough, rich enough, educated enough, good enough.

Self-realization is the integration of every part of you into your wholeness and perfection. Don't make self-realization a job. Don't make applying and living this wisdom a job. Make it a beautiful experience journey that is fun and expansive. The easiest thing is to notice when you are denying a part of yourself, judging a part of yourself. *Just notice.*

You are Source Energy that you focused into a physical body.

"You are Energy. You are consciousness currently focused in physical form for the purpose of joy, expression, expansion, and experiences. You are consciousness exploring the physical realm for the purpose of focused creation and the evolution and expansion of your own Soul, which leads to the expansion and evolution of All That Is."

— THE COUNCIL

You are here in physical form to experience Source Energy in the physical. You are here for the experience of manifestation and creation in physical form, and you are your own greatest creation. Have you ever thought about that? *You are your own greatest creation.*

You focus so much on your external manifestations, and it's understandable why you do. It's enjoyable to you to manifest things that are fun, to manifest experiences, to manifest relationships, to manifest opportunities to live in particular places, and all the wonderful things that you manifest externally, although all is part of your reality and your experience as Creator within your own creation.

You are your own greatest creation. Really take that in for a moment. Look who you have become. Look what you have created. Really, for a moment, come into the realization of who you are and how far you've come and who you have created yourself to be. And it's not about what you haven't created yet. It's not about what you haven't done yet. It's not about what hasn't been healed or fixed yet. It's about you, embracing in this moment, that you are your own greatest creation.

Take a deep breath. Allow yourself in this moment to come fully into your power. Breathe in your power into all of your being. Breathe in the love that you are. Breathe in all that you are. Go within you. Find the still, quiet place of infinite power within you. Feel it. Feel deeply into that place. And as you feel into that place, begin to feel that infinite power within you expanding.

Feel it expanding and getting even brighter. Feel it getting brighter as you go deeper and deeper. And feel the infinite power within you beginning to shine now like the brightest light you've ever seen within you. Feel it shining up to the top of your head and down to the bottoms of your feet and out your fingertips. Feel the infinite power of the bright, beautiful light within you shining so deeply, so brightly, so boldly in every cell of your body. Shine your bright beautiful light through every cell of your body, activating every cell, activating *every* molecule in your body, activating *every* part of you.

Now expand the bright beautiful light that is you one foot around you in every direction—above you, below you, beside you, in front of you, behind you. Focus the infinite power within you into this bright beautiful light that is you, focusing through you one foot around you in every direction. And now fill this room with the bright beautiful light that is you. Focus this infinite power that is you and fill this room with the bright beautiful light of you.

Now expand that bright beautiful light to fill up your whole home with the bright beautiful light that you are. And now expand that light around your home, up, up, up toward the clouds above the trees, up to the birds. Focus the bright beautiful light that you are up above you. And now focus the bright beautiful light that you are down, down, down into the Earth beneath you, into the roots of the trees beneath you, down into the center of the Earth. And expanding up higher again, above the clouds, up toward the moon and up toward the sun and up toward the sky. Higher, higher toward the stars above you as far as you can see throughout all the Universe. Reaching up, reaching up, shining the infinite power of the bright beautiful light that you are.

Now deeper, deeper, deeper into the Earth beneath you. And now expand from you in every direction—to the right, to the left, in front of you, behind you—expand this bright beautiful light that you are all around this planet, all around this beautiful Earth. Shine the infinite power of the bright beautiful light all around you in every direction until there's nowhere that you are not in all the Universe. The power of infinite power within you, the power. You are the infinite power, the power. You are the infinite power, the power. You are the infinite power.

And let this bright, beautiful light that you are shine from within you to every corner of this universe and beyond. Focus it until there is nothing but light. And you are here within the center of your universe, the light that you are, the power that you are. *Oh, it's time to shine. It is time to shine and realize that you are your greatest creation.* Expanding this bright beautiful light that you are, expanding your infinite power. Coming fully into this moment, knowing that you are the most beautiful creation. You are the most important creation. You are your greatest creation. It is you.

As you stand in this moment, shining the bright beautiful light that you are, allow your infinite power to radiate from you, fully allowing the Source Energy that flows through you, fully allowing the Source Energy that is you, fully allowing the Source Energy that is all here for you.

Focus this bright beautiful light that you are into everything, into the ground beneath you, into the Earth beneath you. Focus this bright beautiful light that you are into the grass and into the trees and into the birds and into the bees. Focus this bright beautiful light that you are into the animals, into the trees and the flowers and the mountains and the rivers and the streams and the oceans. Focus this bright beautiful light that you are into the air that you breathe. Focus this bright beautiful light into every human heart. *Focus this bright beautiful light that you are into every human heart.* Focus this bright beautiful light that you are into Oneness with everything. Focus this bright beautiful light until you feel yourself into the *Isness of All That Is* and *Will Ever Be.*

Feel the infinite power that you are and infuse it into bright beautiful light. And as you radiate it from you and feel your way into Oneness with everything, you are the Isness of All That Is and Will Ever Be. It is all here. It is all Source. It is all you. You are your greatest creation. You are your greatest creation. You are your greatest creation. And so it is.

Now go beyond. Go so deeply into this moment that you access every dimension of consciousness, that you feel into everything that is here until you can feel yourself into everything, every dimension, every level, every level of creation within every level of consciousness. Go beyond. *Go beyond,* and bring all that you are and all of creation and all the power of the Source Energy within you into this moment and go deeper.

Go beyond. Go into the realization of all that you are beyond what you have believed yourself to be. Go beyond. Go beyond what you have believed yourself to be. Come into the awareness of you as Creator. Feel yourself moving into the I Am Creator frequency.

Feel yourself as Creator of everything. Feel yourself as Creator everywhere. Feel yourself as Creator within all eternity. Go beyond. Go beyond. Go beyond to the source of the light. Go beyond. Go beyond the light. Go to the source of the light. Go beyond into all of creation and feel it within you. Go beyond. Go as far as you can feel. Expand into it all. And as you do, you realize you are your greatest creation in all the Universe. You are your greatest creation in all the Universe. You are your own greatest creation. And so it is.

Now come back into your body and take a deep breath and feel your body. Feel the light that is still within you. Feel the energy that still flows through you. Take a moment and really, really feel for the truth of this. *You are your own greatest creation.* You are magnificent. You are radiant. You are brilliant. You are Divine.

YOU ARE SOURCE ENERGY FOCUSED IN A PHYSICAL BODY

You're a spiritual being having a human experience. You came forth by your own choosing from an expanded state of consciousness, a higher perspective, a grander viewpoint to experience life in physical form—to experience physical form—because this is the experience that will expand your soul. You came from Source, you will return to Source, Source is what you are. Most people forget that part.

If you've ever been present for the birth of a child or an animal—a horse, kitten, puppy—then you have witnessed the moment when pure Source Energy moved fully into physical form and was birthed into the world. It is an experience that might be described as pure love. You can feel the presence of the Divine. You can witness the miracle.

This was also true when you were born. It was a divine experience when pure Source Energy moved into physical form. But then you forget. You are given a name, you're told you have your dad's nose, your mom's eyes, your grandmother's smile, you're smart like your brother, but not athletic like your sister. You start being compared to other people, and you begin to identify yourself by how others have described you. There are usually not a lot of people who are reminding you daily that you are pure Source Energy focused in physical form, so you begin to associate more with your human description than your true eternal nature.

You came into the human experience for expansion. You came to explore. You came for expression. You came to choose the experiences you want to have for you, and you came to have those experiences.

You are here to awaken to the truth that you are Source Energy that you focused into a physical body. People often enter the awakening process in their life following a near-death experience, a disease or chronic diagnosis, the end of a relationship, the loss of a job, the death of a loved one, or financial devastation. There comes a moment where one no longer identifies with who they thought they were, and they begin to ask the question, "Who am I?"

These are the four most common questions that one seeks to answer when awakening: "Who am I? Why am I here? Where did I come from? Where am I going?" You came from Source, you will return to Source, Source is what you are. You came from the Divine, you will return to the Divine, the Divine is what you are. You came from God, you will return to God, because God is what you are.

You chose to come forth at this time as free, sovereign, divine beings to be on the planet at this time. You came to contribute to the expansion of consciousness because being in physical form will also contribute to your own expansion of consciousness and soul. It is the ultimate privilege and opportunity to come into physical form, to be here at this time during the greatest awakening of human consciousness that has ever occurred, to play, create, and have fun, to do the things that bring you joy, and to allow everything that happens in this experience to contribute to your expansion, to contribute to the expression of all that you are, to allow you the opportunity to look at the different potentials and possibilities and choose from this powerful, awakened, self-realized state to choose the experiences that you want to have for you.

For many people, prior to awakening, they didn't have the awareness to know that you can choose the experiences you want to have for you, to look at all the potentials and possibilities that this life experience in physical form has to offer and say, "Wouldn't it be fun to experience this or experience that?" and then to create your reality.

A student once asked me, "Do souls choose the hardships that some are born into?" In the 11 Spiritual Roles of the Soul course, we discuss the many reasons why a soul incarnates and what roles they are here to play. One of those roles is a transformer. A transformer is someone who comes forth to transform negative patterns that are often generational or ancestral. People in family dynamics often get stuck in the same unconscious patterns of sexual, physical, or emotional abuse, addiction, or negativity. And, because of the learned behaviors that hold one in a lower consciousness and lower vibrational frequency—unknowingly and unconsciously—few if any ever get out of these negative patterns. They just keep being born into the pattern; they carry on the pattern because they aren't consciously aware of anything different.

A transformer might say, "No more. This pattern stops with me. I know I am Source. I know I am God. I know I am the Divine. I'm going to go forth into a human experience and I am going to transform that negativity or, better said, unconscious pattern or behavior, and I am going to create a new story of the love, consciousness, compassion, abundance, and well-being. I am going to bring consciousness and the love. I am creating a new path, a new way forward for myself and anyone else who is ready and choosing."

I have tremendous reverence for souls that choose to incarnate as transformers. They are courageous, wise souls with a great love for humanity. You too came forth as Source Energy into a physical body because of your great love. You might feel that great love for people, animals, or nature, or you might feel a great love for raising the consciousness and vibration on the planet.

When you remember who you really are, why you are here, where you came from, and where you're going—you have the greatest wisdom on the planet. The secret's revealed. There's no more illusion. You know who you are. You know why you're here. You know you are Source, you will return to Source, Source is what you are.

You are the Creator within your own creation of reality.

"You are Creator within your own creation of reality, and it is here, and it is now, and you are free. You are free to create the reality that you choose for you, and you're free to experience it now, and you're free to be here, now."

— THE COUNCIL

You are the Creator of your reality. You have many more levels of creation to explore, to expand into, and to experience. As you move into higher levels of consciousness, more becomes available to you. It gets easier. It gets lighter. It gets better. It flows. There is more magic. There are more miracles. There's more fun. There's more play, and there's *no end to creation.*

There is no end to creating the reality that you want to experience for you at the highest level. But it is a choice that you make every day with what you're focused on, the meaning you're giving it, and the level of consciousness you're in, which allows vibration and frequency to be elevated and expanded into your natural state, which is joyful and inspired and full of vitality, and coming to a place where you live so wholly and completely within yourself that the power that you are draws to you magic, miracles, and manifestations that you never experience the lack of.

There is freedom in letting go of all that you're attached to, of all that creates resistance and judgment and the feeling of overwhelm within you. But we're not talking about the kind of letting go that is passive, where you are just going to let go and wait around and be patient and maybe something will happen if you just let go. No.

It's the *letting go* that is connecting you to Oneness consciousness. In the moment that you intentionally let go, you powerfully move into the state of Oneness consciousness where anything and everything is possible for you, and you begin to play in the multidimensional realities that are available to you as you create in multiple dimensions of consciousness that are presenting themselves to you more and more every day if you're paying attention and you're willing to play.

Creating is playing. Playing is creating. There is so much freedom in knowing that there is no end to creation ever, that you are always creating and recreating your reality. It's going to be really important that you stay in joy, stay in a playful, lighthearted, creative, inspired, innocent vibration, because you are literally taking quantum leaps forward in releasing density, trauma, drama, old stories, old energy, and old beliefs.

You might be feeling like you are in a new state of consciousness, you are feeling better, you are feeling more joyful, you are feeling more freedom, and yet your reality hasn't taken the quantum leap forward that you wish it had. Your reality hasn't taken that quantum leap forward into the new potentials and possibilities, but we assure you that it will in rapid time. You will leapfrog into new realities. It will be a quantum leap. But it is not of the human's doing.

It is not of the human's doing. It is not the human figuring it out. It is not your human making it happen. It is not your human forcing your desires. It is not your human forcing energy where your human thinks it should go. It is you letting yourself go into your natural state of God consciousness, which is always available to you, and playing and creating and having fun in these new realities from that level.

CREATE IN NEW ENERGY

You must understand that, as you move into higher dimensions of consciousness, many of those dimensions—those dimensions above the 5th Dimension—are formless realities. You're experiencing formless creation, True Creation that is formless, which allows the highest potential and possibility to then filter down into the lower dimensions of consciousness where you experience form.

You want new energy, you want new consciousness, you want a New Earth reality, and yet you want to keep creating those in old energy, which is why you asked the question, why is it that I don't feel like my life is taking a quantum leap forward into new realities; it looks like it's the same? Because you're still trying to create it with old energy. You're trying to push old energy where you think it should go.

You've never been *here*—to this level of consciousness—before in physical form, which is why it feels like you don't really know what you want anymore, or you're almost exhausted desiring the things you've been wanting for so long. Now, all the laws of creation and the laws of attraction and the laws of gestation still work in every dimension of consciousness, but you are the pioneer, and you are the trailblazer through this new level of consciousness that is now available to you. It is here and it is now, and now it's about the journey through these higher levels of consciousness.

You are in an experience where living mastery is what you are looking for, desiring, seeking. You are asking to live this mastery. You are asking to live at these higher levels of consciousness. You're asking to live and allow all the energy that is here for you.

Your human is not going to do that. Your human is not going to figure that out. Your human is not going to make that happen. Your human, at this point, is along for the ride, along for the journey, here to have fun and to play and to create and to marvel in the magnificence of practical magic presenting itself to you all day long—Divine orchestration, synchronicities, coincidences that happen faster and more fully and more vividly and with more energy—and creating your reality, the creation of reality.

Much of what you're asking about, much of where you are now, much of which you desire to experience next is new levels of creating your reality. The creation of reality. All the energy is here. All the energy is yours. The energy is never created nor destroyed. It changes form. And it's all here for you.

Consciousness and your awareness are what open you up and allow you into a state where energy is flowing to you and through you, and you are fully in the God consciousness where all the energy came from. The consciousness of God, the God consciousness, all the energy that is here for you, combined with you in the state of awareness that you are the Creator within your own creation, is going to move you into levels of reality and creating your reality beyond anything you have ever experienced so far.

And when you're feeling yourself in what might appear to be a fight between old and new, you have unintentionally or potentially unknowingly moved yourself down into lower levels of consciousness with an awareness of new energy but where you are still trying to create with old energy.

You are totally and completely free in every way to create your reality however you wish it to be. That means if you have a job that you don't like or a relationship that you don't like or a living situation that you don't like or a money situation that you don't like or a situation with your body that you don't like, you are totally and completely free to create the reality that you want to choose for you, that you want to create for you, that you want to experience for you.

BEYOND CIRCUMSTANCES AND INTO CONSCIOUSNESS

There is nothing stopping you except your human. There's nothing holding you back except your human that doesn't know who he or she is. If you really let yourself go into God consciousness—because the truth is that the human, on some level, knows the power of the God consciousness, of Oneness, of knowing that you are Creator within your own creation—your human feels like it loses control. And yet you're free. And yet you think you have no control.

All you need to do is go above and beyond these circumstances and these conditions into a consciousness, an awareness where you know there is a higher perspective here, there is a grand plan, there is a better feeling than whatever it was that was tripping you up or creating the disharmony or upsetting you. And all you need do is allow yourself into that place. But your human, your beloved human—we love *your human* so much—still wants to control and run the show. But so much of what the human wants is so limited, still based in lack and old energy because that's all the human knows.

The human only knows how to have a job and earn and force and effort and do and do and do. The human only knows to fight and argue and point out where someone else is making you feel bad. The human only knows how to try to force and fix and make the body be different. The human only knows really the 3rd and 4th Dimensions of consciousness.

And there's nothing wrong with this. You are a pioneer. You are a trailblazer. You are a wayshower. You're here for the higher levels of consciousness. You're here to create new realities. You're here to expand the potential and the possibilities for humankind. You are in the metamorphosis of birthing yourself into new levels of consciousness and fully allowing the new energy that is available to you.

Now, energy was never really created nor destroyed. Because of this, it's not that old energy and new energy are necessarily separate, but that new energy is you experiencing the God consciousness, the awareness that you are the Creator within your own creation, knowing yourself as the God that you are, free, sovereign, perfect, powerful, divine, brilliant, magnificent. That is what you are. No one outside of you can make you that. No job can make you that. No level of success can make you that. No philanthropic endeavor can make you that because you already are.

So, when you feel stuck or not as far ahead as you want to be, remember that your human is still grasping onto lower dimensions of consciousness, trying to force it and figure it out and make it happen. The things that you feel so entangled in and responsible for and held back by and upset by don't really matter. You probably won't even think of these things a month from now or a year from now or three years from now, which is how we know for sure that they don't really matter as much as you're making these things matter.

They are just ways that your human keeps you in lower dimensions of consciousness because it doesn't know how it will maintain control over everything it thinks it's responsible for when you let yourself go fully into the consciousness of God, into the truth of who you really are, into the experience of Creator within your own creation.

Allow yourself. Just let go. Now imagine yourself sitting in the most beautiful paradise, white sand beaches, bright turquoise blue water, sunshine on your face, the most perfect breeze gently touching your cheek and your skin, hearing the gentle waves as they wash onto the beach, gazing at the beautiful foliage and the flowers and the trees, the colors and the shapes, looking around you at the perfection and the beauty. And as you gaze out over the water there are dolphins playing in the water.

You can hear them. You can see them jumping and playing and dancing together. And the water is so clear that you can see the fish of all different colors and all different sizes swimming in the water. You might even notice a sea turtle or a whale.

As you begin to notice all around you there's the beautiful sound of nature in perfect harmony, a sound so sweet and so beautiful, it's like the perfect melody. How sweet the sound. And as you feel the sand beneath your feet, your whole body feels so perfectly warm and radiant in the sun. You feel such deep vitality and well-being. It is the most pristine paradise, and you created it. And as you sit in your perfect paradise, Creator within your own creation, you are there in the reality that you yourself have created, and it feels so good. It's paradise, and it's reality, and you created it all.

As you sit in your paradise that you have created, you can play and expand in any reality you choose. Go to your paradise. And as you feel your body, notice how beautiful your body is. Notice how handsome. Notice how strong. Notice that your body is almost glowing, that there is a light within your body that radiates from you.

Go into your body and make it full of vitality and longevity. Make your skin glow. Make your eyes bright and beautiful. Make your hair feel soft and even flowing. And dress your body in the most perfect expression of you. Maybe a long, beautiful, white gown or a bright, colorful dress, or a T-shirt and some shorts and some flip-flops. You're the master. You get to choose. Create your body. Create the reality of your beautiful body. And focus into your body until you can feel fun in your body. It feels so fun and playful to be in a body.

Now in your paradise you jump up and maybe you run into the waves and swim out to the dolphins and dive in and play and swim and dance with the dolphins. Or maybe you run along the beach as fast as you can with the wind blowing through your hair. You are free.

You are free. Run. Run. Run. Or maybe you simply reach your hands up toward the sun and just feel every cell in your body illuminate in the light, free, glowing, beautiful, powerful, handsome, strong.

Then maybe you go back out, dive in the water, dive all the way down to swim with the fishes and dance and play with the dolphins. You are Creator of your reality. And as you play and create and swim and dance and run on the beach in this perfect paradise, you realize you are rich. There is abundance everywhere. Wealth, prosperity, reflected to you in everything. The fruit, the vegetables, the trees, the sand, the water, everything around you is reflecting your abundance to you. You have everything you could ever want and need, and all you need do is think of something fun to experience or create and it is there. No delay. No having to go make more money. You just focus on any reality you want to experience.

As you sit on the beach maybe you desire a delicious meal served on a golden platter, the most amazing foods, all of your favorite things, and it's all delivered to you as you sit on the beach and enjoy a feast of abundance. All you need do is focus, and it comes to you. And as you're sitting on the beach enjoying your beautiful meal in paradise, once again you focus on the sound. And as you do, you focus on the sweet melody, and music begins to play. And as the music begins to play, you find yourself dancing on the beach, dancing with the waves, dancing all around. And as you dance, suddenly there is someone there dancing with you, smiling and looking in your eyes.

As you dance, feeling the sunshine on your face, you are free, you are together, you are playing and creating. They are here in your reality with you. Look into their eyes, feel their skin. There's so much love, so much joy, so much excitement. You are dancing together. They are here in your reality on this beach with you in your paradise that you created, and you drew them here into your reality. And as you dance and play in the waves and dine on your delicious meal and then jump into the water together and swim out to play with the dolphins, looking in their eyes, seeing into their soul, they are God, as are you. They are Creator, as are you. You're experiencing creation. You are creating your reality.

As you allow yourself to be here for one more moment, take it in. You just created reality in paradise with your beautiful body and your abundant prosperity and your love. You are Creator within your own creation of reality, and it is here, and it is now, and you are free. You are free to create the reality that you choose for you, and you're free to experience it now, and you're free to be here, now.

Take one more moment, really feel it, and then move yourself easily and effortlessly back into this moment. Come back fully into your body and feel that same feeling about your body that you did in your paradise. Feel the same feeling of freedom, of abundance and prosperity, and of love. Bring it all here into your body, into this reality. Really feel it. Feel it all the way down into your toes and into your fingertips. Feel it in the crown of your head and in your shoulders and in your spine, down the backs of your legs. Feel it everywhere.

You are Creator. Say it with us. "I am Creator within my own creation. I am Creator within my own creation. I am Creator within my own creation. I create my reality. I am Creator. I am Creator, and I am free. I am free. I am free."

Take a deep breath. We invite you to spend as much time as possible in your paradise. The more you allow yourself into higher dimensions of consciousness, where the new energy flows to you freely and fully, all else will be done through you, through your consciousness, through your allowing of energy to support you.

Play in your paradise. Play in your Heaven on Earth. Create it every day. Create your paradise every day. Create your Heaven on Earth every day. Create it and recreate it and create it and recreate it and create it and recreate it every day.

You will experience an expansion of your physical reality like nothing you've ever experienced before. You will experience an expansion of your consciousness like nothing you've ever experienced before. You are going to see an expansion of your life experience in ways you've never dreamed of, in your relationships, in your body, in your finances, in your potential, in your intuition, in your inspiration, and in your intelligence.

You can create any reality that you choose for you. If you will just do your part to focus yourself into pure love, paradise, your Heaven on Earth—the energy will do the rest. Your job is the consciousness and the awareness. Energy will do the rest. It will expand everything for you.

You're going to expand into realities, in new experiences that are going to be so incredible for you, so magical, so loving, so beautiful, so abundant, your human will hardly be able to stand without falling to your knees with reverence for the power that is the real you, for reverence to the perfection of God, to witnessing the divine plan unfolding right before your eyes.

Just let go. That's all that's asked of you. Don't try to control this. Don't try to control anything. Don't try to control anyone. You're going to see the difference between control and Divine orchestration. You're going to see the difference between control and magic. We can't even call it practical because it's going to be fuller and more fun and more amazing than what you've ever thought is practical.

Let go and have fun and expand and play and create. This time is going to expand everything, creating anew on every level within your reality. And all you need do is allow yourself into your paradise. Whether it's on a beautiful beach or a mountaintop or next to a stream, it's all perfect. But go there. Move yourself into the reality that you want to create for you right here and now. Create it and recreate it every day as often as possible.

Get excited about new levels of creating your reality. Get excited about living your highest potential. Get excited about realizing yourself as Creator within your own creation. Get excited about living as the embodied, realized master that you are, and living *this mastery* that is you. Get excited about being the pioneer and the trailblazer, the wayshower, that you are.

There's so much more. It just gets better. It's time to witness the magnificent expansion into your highest potential. Allow, allow, allow. Allow yourself to play. Allow yourself to have fun. Allow yourself into paradise.

YOU ARE CREATOR WITHIN YOUR OWN CREATION

The Council says there is one answer to every question: "You are Creator within your own creation." And *everyone else* is too.

In 2006, I was 26 years old and diagnosed with melanoma, a cancer that was spreading rapidly throughout my body. I was newly married, and I had a demanding corporate career at that time. I had multiple biopsies, multiple surgeries, and after two years of *fighting* the cancer, it had metastasized back in its original location, which was a grave diagnosis.

My doctor was frustrated. I think we all were. I was worn down and devastated facing my own potential mortality at such a young age. I was preparing for my sixth surgery when my doctor came in the room, pulled up a chair beside me and said, "Sara, there's nothing I can do for you. This is coming from within you, and you're the only one that can stop it."

I believe this was a divinely orchestrated moment. It was not a common thing for any doctor to say. Immediately after saying those words to me, the doctor left the room. As I sat there all alone repeating in my head what he had said to me, *I knew* that I had unconsciously created the cancer in my body. And I had created it as a way out of the human experience so that I didn't have to leave my marriage. I created cancer in my own body to die so that I didn't have to go through a painful, emotional, devastating divorce.

It was a moment that might be referred to as an epiphany. I didn't feel scared or any judgment about my newfound awareness. I felt surrounded by my guides, my angels, my brother who had transitioned. I felt safe. I felt loved. I did not have any judgment for myself. I did not have any judgment for anyone else. I had complete and total awareness and the realization that I had created this entire situation.

I also knew that I wanted to live and that I would be cured. I knew I had to get through the surgery and then get divorced. I felt complete and total clarity. And most importantly, I knew if I could unconsciously create cancer, I would consciously heal my body and create the life I did want.

I went in and had that last surgery. From that point in time, I have never had another occurrence of melanoma almost two decades later. I healed up from that surgery, and I did what was one of the hardest things I'd ever done in my life, which was leave my marriage. It was the catalyst to changing my entire life and asking the question, what is my purpose and how do I live it?

AWAKENING YOUR CONSCIOUSNESS

People often say when hearing they create their own reality, "If I create my own reality, then you're saying that someone who has cancer created that?" With great compassion and kindness, I offer that no one would *ever* consciously, intentionally create disease in their body, create traumatic, dramatic situations, create a terrible car accident, or create a lifelong injury. No one would ever consciously, intentionally create that. But sometimes, people have deeply emotional unconscious fears as I did. These things are not meant to kill you, but awaken you to live more consciously, come into your power, and create the life you do want, even if that means navigating through major change.

No one would ever *choose* a traumatic experience where someone was physically, emotionally, sexually abusive, or violent. You did not *cause* those things to happen to you.

Violence, war, crime, and abuse occur when someone is in the belief of their own separation and commits acts of violence against other people out of their own fear, lack, limitation, and total separation from the love that they are and the love of another. To understand this, it's helpful to understand different levels of consciousness.

You are *never* going to rid the 3rd Dimension of separation of fear, lack, limitation, war, violence, abuse, or suffering. It is your opportunity to *elevate yourself* out of the illusion of separation, out of the 3rd Dimension, which is such a heavy, dense vibration that we experience struggle and suffering. When you elevate yourself out of fear, lack, limitation, and separation, things such as abuse, war, and violence are no longer part of *your experience.*

It is not about bypassing anything, it's about elevating your consciousness and understanding that there are different levels of *consciousness*. You are Source Energy here focused in physical form, you chose to come forth to remember who you are and why you're here, and then *elevate yourself into the 5th Dimension of pure love.*

When you come fully into self-realization, you are whole, complete, and the past is healed. Why? Because you have elevated yourself into the consciousness of pure love and transcended separation and the illusion of lack, limitation, and fear. If you are someone who was abused, violated, or someone committed a crime against you, you are *not* responsible for that. However, in *this moment,* you are responsible for the state of consciousness *you are in.* You are choosing in this moment what reality you will create here and now.

You have the ability to create your reality. And not only that, but you're *always* creating your reality. The level of consciousness you are in is what is creating your reality in this moment. When you accept that you are totally and completely responsible, from this moment on, for creating your reality the way you want it to be, you enter a new awareness and begin to understand that you are Creator within your own creation of reality. You will discover the freedom that you have to create your reality the way you want it to be. When you take total responsibility, from *this moment,* for creating your reality, you instantly manifest the freedom to create your reality the way you want it to be.

What you focus on, and the meaning you give it, is what creates your reality.

"You can tell yourself any story you choose because you are Creator within your own creation of your reality, and what you focus on and the meaning you're giving it is what is creating your reality."

— THE COUNCIL

Your thoughts affect your emotions. Your emotions affect the way that you feel. The way that you feel is what is determining the level of vibration and consciousness you're in, which is determining the level of reality that you are allowing and how closely you are to True Creation. It starts with the thoughts that you are thinking. And all emotion comes from thoughts. It is the thoughts that you are thinking about anything that are creating the emotion. It's the stories you're telling yourself. You can tell yourself any story you choose because you are Creator within your own creation of your reality. What you focus on and the meaning you're giving it is what is creating your reality.

As you focus on something and you think that life is really good and this is a really powerful time and this is an amazing time and heavenly miracles are coming your way and new levels of creation are opening up to you and it's going to be better than you ever thought it was, well, you'll notice when you think thoughts like that and tell yourself stories like that, it feels really good. Your emotions feel very good. You feel high. You feel good. You feel excited. You're excited about your life. You're in that vibration where you're open to surprises and delight and magic and miracles, and amazing things can present themselves to you.

You could also be telling yourself a story where you're not good enough, you haven't done enough *yet*, so-and-so should have done more for you, so-and-so should have done this for you, so-and-so shouldn't have done that to you, and the world isn't the way it should be, and these people are wrong, and this needs to get fixed, and nothing's ever working out for you, and the money's not there, and your body is too old or too painful or too this, and you can tell yourself *that* story and you'll notice it feels pretty awful, doesn't it? It's your truth, it's your story, it's your reality, you are creating it.

The thoughts that you are thinking come from your consciousness, come from your thoughts that are on automatic pilot just rolling around like a hamster on a wheel. They're the stories you keep telling. They're the same meaning you keep giving to things that lead to emotions that feel imbalanced and unpleasant to you. You've got to stop. You have the power to come into the moment because all of your power is in the now moment. When you come into the moment in your power and you put space around you, when you slow everything down and you come into the power of you in this moment and the power of your thoughts and the power of your consciousness and the power of you as Creator within your own creation and you choose the story you wish to tell yourself, you focus upon the things that are good for you and you focus on giving them meaning that is supportive to you, and you will find yourself feeling your way into new levels of consciousness and reality where heavenly miracles present themselves to you every day, all day long.

These are not the sort of miracles your human can figure out. We're talking the *really big stuff*, God-level miracles, because you yourself are an alchemist of light and love, and as you step fully into your mastery, into the embodied, enlightened, ascended master that you are and live as the embodied master that you are here on Earth, you come into the realization that everything is Source, and energy is in everything. Consciousness is what moves energy into form, and it is your consciousness that is directing energy. It is your consciousness that is creating. Energy is responding to you.

YOU ARE NOT YOUR STORIES

You are a force field of consciousness made up of particles of infinite creation that are always responding to you, and as you remember that you can come into this state of knowing the power you have, that you can alchemize anything back into love and light, you can give it to the light. Let it go to the light. You can give it to the light and let it be recreated through love, through light aligned with truth. This is the power you have.

The stories about your childhood are not who you are. What has happened to you in your life is not the truth of who you are. Your failures, your mistakes, they don't matter. They're not you. They're not the truth of you. They're not what's really going on here. The things that you feel victimized by, the places where you feel power-less, are not the truth of you.

You are a divine, sovereign, infinite being of light and love. You are an ascended master focused in the human experience. You are here to embody the ascended, enlightened master being that you are, to live fully awakened, fully conscious, fully aligned in the human experience; living fully, loving fully, and being all that you are. And nothing that is of lack and limitation is the truth of you. Nothing that is of fear and separation is the truth of you.

Your consciousness is the most important thing in all situations. If the money isn't there, if the well-being isn't there, if the relation-ship is struggling, it is all about elevating your consciousness. This is the answer to everything, because you are Creator within your own creation. When you go to the highest levels of consciousness as the Creator that you are within your own creation, you begin to open to and allow heavenly miracles, God-level miracles, opportunities for the impossible, for the infinite potentials and pure possibilities that are here available to you to move through into your experience. This is the power you have.

You're going to go to a whole new level of relationships, health, well-being, your relationship with your body, your finances, your work in the world, your service, your career, your vocations. Every single one of you absolutely has the power to attract to you the infinite resources that are here for you for the fulfillment of any inspiration or desired creation. You can create through an experience of True Creation without an agenda and without ever experiencing the lack and the limitation of anything while also desiring, focusing, and expanding into more—more potentials, more possibilities, more experiences, more magic, more miracles, more love, more well-being, more abundance, more freedom, more beauty. That is why you are *here*. This is the journey. And you're ready yet again to step up into another level, into another level of manifestation and creation, and experience an expansion, an expression and existence, and it really, really matters.

You are here in this human experience during the greatest transformation of human consciousness that has ever occurred in any lifetime and you chose to come forth as a wayshower at this time to show others the way into higher levels of consciousness, to bring higher levels of consciousness into the physical Earth plane, to expand the potentials and the possibilities, to come fully into realization and live as the embodied master that you are and stay on the planet at this time because you *know* how important it is.

Every day, every moment is the opportunity for you to fully step into your power and live your purpose and be the embodiment of the truth of who you are. And yet the only thing that keeps you from doing this is believing in your unworthiness, getting distracted, staying in states of unconsciousness, allowing your thoughts to run the show, and allowing the old stories to just recreate the same unwanted experiences time and time again.

You are so powerful. You are so loved. The entire Company of Heaven is here guiding you, loving you, inspiring you, cocreating with you. The abundance of Heaven on Earth is here and available to you, and heavenly miracles are the truth of you. You have this power in every area of your life to live it to the fullest, to come into the grander perspective of the truth of who you are, and live your life in the highest realms of consciousness and the highest realms of creation while still fully present, in your power, in a physical form.

It's more important than ever before that you find peace within you and harmony within you and abundance within you and love within you and joy within you and freedom within you and beauty within you and fun. Your collective human consciousness is going through the greatest transformation that has ever occurred at a rapid pace and it's possible because of you, because of your consciousness, because you have awakened to the truth of who you are. And while it is not your responsibility to choose for any other or the collective as a whole, it is your responsibility to choose for you, to take full and total responsibility for you and your life and your thoughts and your emotions and your feelings and your creations and your manifestations, because nothing has ever and will ever and can ever go wrong.

There is data and information in every experience. It is always understood that this is a journey through consciousness. This is a journey into higher levels of consciousness. This is a journey through dimensions of consciousness. You think you're walking down the road. You think you're driving to where you think you need to go. You are on a journey through dimensions of consciousness in a physical form. There is nothing better than that, we assure you. You're on a journey through dimensions of consciousness while being able to see and taste and touch and hear and smell and think and create and manifest and love and play and experience joy and fun. Oh, how good it is.

EVERYTHING IS POTENTIAL AND POSSIBILITY

In the sea of endless potential and possibility, you will ultimately focus upon certain things. The meaning you then give those things you are focused upon creates your experience of reality. What you focus on, and the meaning you give it, is what creates your reality.

Take a simple example of a pen. You might have several pens on your desk to write with, but let's say in this example you have one pen that you choose when you sit down to write. To anyone else it might be a seemingly meaningless pen. However, if the pen was given to you by someone special as a gift, that pen now has more meaning. If it was the last gift your loved one gave you before they passed away, it might be even more meaningful to you. If you think of your loved one each time you use the pen and feel a sense of closeness and connection with your loved one when writing with it, now you have created your experience.

Another example would be the perspective of two people who have the same experience, like siblings. One sibling might remember an event from childhood completely different than the other sibling. One might have focused on one aspect of the experience, given it a positive meaning, and therefore, remembers the experience positively. While the other sibling might have focused on something different, giving it an entirely different meaning, and recall the experience as being negative.

Everything is potential and possibility. Everything is essentially neutral. You can look at something as a potential and possibility that is exciting to you. Someone else might not have ever focused on that thing their entire life. It's just not a potential or a possibility that they're interested in. And someone else could have focused on it from a very different perspective and given it a very different meaning than you have. Either way, you're creating your reality.

Another perspective might be how people see the world. Do you live in a loving, supportive, beautiful, peaceful world, or is the world hostile, dangerous, scary, and full of suffering? If you are focused on the difficulties and struggles of life, and the meaning you're giving to life is that it's difficult and a struggle, you will perceive more and more difficulties and struggles. You will draw more experiences of struggle and difficulty to create a reality where life is difficult and a struggle. And if you focus on the peace, kindness, and love in the world, you will create a reality where you experience more peace, kindness, and love.

One of my favorite examples that The Council has given over the years is to focus on a tree in your neighborhood. Now imagine it was planted by some significant or prominent figure in history, like Abraham Lincoln, Martin Luther King Jr., Jesus, Shakespeare, Gandhi, or Queen Elizabeth II. Now, suddenly, this tree is not just an ordinary tree like all the other trees. It's a special tree—a sacred tree. Your experience is totally different when you change your focus and the meaning you give this tree.

You can take any average, ordinary thing, and you can focus on it as pure potential and possibility. It is here to help you in creating your reality. It is here for you. You give all things a meaning that inspires you, empowers you, uplifts you, excites you, and is meaningful to you.

Channeled Activation on Expanding Your Perspective

We are so pleased and delighted to have the opportunity to speak with you all on this fine and glorious day indeed. While our words to you are important, this is a vibrational experience of remembering the truth of who you really are, why you are here, and all that you intended when you chose this magnificent life experience, because we assure you, your life is meant to be so very good for you.

You are here as Creator creating your reality. You are here as Creator, embodying all that you are. You are here as Creator on a magnificent journey, a grand adventure. You are here to experience all that you are.

There are no words that could ever fully describe all that you are. It is something that you feel. You are a feeling being. Truth often expresses itself in a deep feeling or knowing of truth, even if it is something you have never heard before, even if it is something that goes against all you have ever believed yourself to be.

The truth of who you are can never quite be put into words that will satisfy your human mind. We invite you to ask the question and allow the feeling, ask the question and allow the feeling. As you go through your day, ask the question. Allow your awareness. Allow yourself to perceive beyond what you have ever deemed yourself to be. Allow yourself to experience all that you are and the truth of you in a new way. The question: Who am I? Who am I? Who am I?

Whatever you feel as you ask yourself that question, whatever awareness comes to you, in whatever ways you begin to perceive yourself, know yourself, and experience yourself—while words are important, it is the feeling. I Am. I Am. I am the Creator frequency. I am light. I am love. I am Creator. I am the Isness of All That Is.

As you allow awarenesses to expand your perspective, you begin to experience who you really are, the power you have to create your reality as Creator within your own creation, because we assure you, you are everything you wish to be, you already are, it is all within you, it always will be. You are magnificent. You are brilliant. You are the perfection of Source Itself here in physical form on this grand adventure. Life is meant to be fun. It is meant to be lived fully. You are here to love fully and be all that you are.

There is something within your heart, no matter what your life experience has been until now, no matter what has ever occurred, there is something within your heart that knows. It knows there is a state of consciousness, a place, a reality that you are here to experience, where you are whole and worthy and complete, a reality where you experience abundance, love, well-being, joy, freedom, beauty, fulfillment, meaning.

There is something within your heart that knows you are here to realize all that you are. You are here to realize your masterpiece. You are here to create your vision of Heaven on Earth. You are here to experience the pure love that is your reality if it is your choosing, because pure love is the truth of who you really are.

We are always with you. We are always available to you. We love you, we love you, we love you. And with that, we are complete.

Review: Expanding Your Perspective

Success Principle #1: You are everything you wish to be. You already are.

- You have everything you need within you—and an infinite supply of resources available to you—to create the life of your dreams.

- Nothing could ever threaten your worth. Nothing you do can make you more worthy.

SUCCESS PRINCIPLE #2: You are Source Energy that you focused into a physical body.

- You have come here by your own choosing from an expanded state of consciousness to experience life in physical form.

- Choose whatever term feels most aligned to you: Source, God, the Divine, Spirit, Soul, Creator.

SUCCESS PRINCIPLE #3: You are the Creator within your own creation of reality.

- This is the answer to every question you could ask.

- Remember that everyone else is also Creator within their own creation.

SUCCESS PRINCIPLE #4: What you focus on, and the meaning you give it, is what creates your reality.

- Everything is potential and possibility.

- Choose from this moment to be completely responsible for your life.

PART II

EXPERIENCING YOUR LIFE

"You are here to live your grand adventure.
You are here to live the most extraordinary existence of
human life, whatever that means for you. You are here to expand the
potentials and the possibilities that exist for all of humankind. You
are here to fully awaken to the truth of who you are, to come into
realization, to integrate every part of you, and then to live as the
embodied, enlightened master that you are, that you are here to be.

"Your presence in physical form on the planet at this time is so
very important. And you are invited in every moment and in every
opportunity and in everything that presents itself to you to elevate
the consciousness, to go beyond, to expand what is possible, to
see from a grander perspective, to bring a new awareness,
to raise the vibration, to raise the frequency. Everything
is your opportunity, dear master."

— THE COUNCIL

These success principles will help you to create an experience of more ease, flow, peace, and joy in your life. When you take each of these success principles and apply them in your life, it provides you with the answer and solution to any challenge that you might be facing. These principles empower you to navigate your daily life with greater harmony and a sense of purpose.

A common question that I receive is, "What is my purpose and how do I live it?" We often struggle to answer this question and seek to discover our own gifts and how to share them with the world. These principles also support you in living your purpose and sharing your unique gifts.

First and foremost, *that is* your gift to the world. Your light, your love, who you are, the experiences you've had, what you enjoy, what you believe in, how you show up, the twinkle in your eye, the smile on your face, the joy in your heart—is your purpose and that is your gift to the world. Your gift is your whole, healed, happy, healthy self!

Nothing will stop you from doing what you are called to do, when you are called to do it. Nothing is going to stop you from doing what it is you're called to do, create, share, or put into the world. You might experience doubts, fears, or uncertainty, but within you there will be clarity, energy, and a *knowing* that will propel you forward.

Be gentle to yourself. Remember that *you are* the gift. Your life is your platform. *Your life is your platform!* Your life will lead you to your gifts and guide you to how you wish to share them with others. The characteristics that you most want for others will help you to discover what you value most in life. When you know what you value, what you are passionate about, what you want to share, momentum moves you with ease and flow toward the experiences and opportunities for you to use your life as the platform for sharing your experiences, excitement, abilities, and enthusiasm.

If you most want the people you love to experience a life of peace, well-being, and harmony, these things are likely characteristics that *you value*. If you most want the people you care about to experience love, self-love, or worthiness, these are things that you value. If you want the people you love to experience abundance, freedom, and fulfillment, then these are likely what you value.

What do you value most? What is *your* passion? How do you use your life as the platform for being the essence of that passion and expressing what you most value? If you feel called to write a book, start a podcast, create your own course, paint, do photography, study history, volunteer at an animal sanctuary—do it, enjoy it, have fun with it! It will lead you to your calling, your purpose, and your gifts.

People often feel like they are not enough or that there is something they are supposed to do. If there is, you will discover it through your joy, passion, excitement, curiosity, and enthusiasm for what you value in life. Nothing will stop you from doing what you're called to do when you're called to do it. Your life is your platform. Be gentle to yourself.

These are the success principles for experiencing life, creating peace and ease, and experiencing more ease and flow in your life. It's all here for you. And who doesn't want more of that?

Everything is always happening for you, not to you.

"Everything is bringing you into a new level of power so that you can choose the reality that you want to create for you."

— THE COUNCIL

When you remember that everything is happening for you, not to you, you will come back into your power. You will open back up. You will start to see the potentials and possibilities. You will get back in alignment with the flow. You can let energy and light guide the way, and it will be choiceless. It will be easy, and it will be effortless, and it will be harmonious, and it will be expeditious.

You are asked to show up as love and consciousness in action, and to be all that you are, and to be in *your truth,* and set *yourself* tree. Know that the Universe is always conspiring in your highest and best good, in your favor. Everything is always happening for you, not to you, to bring you into new levels of your power.

If someone hurts your feelings, someone disappoints you, someone lets you down, someone makes a mistake, someone does something to you, and you notice that you are feeling frustrated, stuck, like things aren't working out, aren't moving forward, or like you've made a mistake—stop. The most important thing for you to choose in that moment is to know that *this* is happening for you. It's happening for you.

The thing that's not moving is happening for you. The thing that's changing is happening for you. The thing that's ending is happening for you. The thing that's beginning is happening for you. The person that's showing up is happening for you. The person that's not showing up is happening for you.

Are *you* in your power? Because when you are perceiving that something is happening *to you* and you are feeling resistance, reactiveness, and pushing against *what is*, you're not in your power. You can tell by the way that you feel when you're not in your power. You can tell when you're frustrated and fighting against. When you are warring against anything outside of you, you are warring with every cell within you. You are pushing against and fighting *within you*. There is no *out there* like you think it is. It first goes through you.

Even if you think you're fighting some greater cause out there, all that energy must first go through you. Your body doesn't know you intend to focus that fight outside of you. Your body and the cells of your body are focused into a vibrational state of fight, war, attack. When you're fighting against anyone or anything, that energy is going through you first.

When you know that everything is happening for you, bringing you into new levels of your power, you can observe what is happening without entangling. There will be clarity and confidence that will come from any situation as you view it from this perspective. An important certainty will come from these experiences, and things will become choiceless.

As you stand in your power, stand in your clarity, stand in your confidence, and choose that this is happening for you, you will begin to be more aware of why certain events or experiences are happening for you. It might take time to see the gifts that came from what appeared to be an unwanted or unfortunate situation. Ask yourself, "Is it possible that something good could come from this? Is it possible there could be a gift in all of this?" When you start to focus on why it is happening for you, you begin to uncover many more potentials and possibilities.

Whatever it is, it's happening for your highest and best good. Whatever it is, it's happening *for you*. Whatever it is, it's serving in your self-realization so that you can step into greater levels of love and consciousness, which will raise your vibration, which will begin a tremendous momentum that allows you to be the most powerful

Creator within your own creation. You will begin to summon new potentials and possibilities that might just manifest in the most magical, amazing, exciting, and spontaneous ways!

FALLING INTO PLACE, NOT FALLING APART

In 2008, I felt like my entire life was falling apart. I had just gone through a nearly two-year battle with cancer. My marriage had ended. The stock market had crashed. The real estate market had crashed. I no longer felt comfortable in the house I had built and once loved but couldn't sell it due to a down market. My company had been sold and my future was uncertain. I was in the beginning of what I would later discover was *my awakening.* While it seemed like everything was falling apart, what I couldn't see at the time was that everything was falling into place and being Divinely orchestrated for me to discover who I really was and how I wanted to create my life.

One of my favorite quotes is from Steve Jobs: "You can't connect the dots looking forward; you can only connect them looking backward. So you have to trust that the dots will connect in your future." It's only when you come to a place in your life and you look back that you see that some greater power was orchestrating everything in your life, bringing you to this moment, awakening you to more. Everything is always happening for you, not to you. Things aren't falling apart. Things are falling into place for you.

There is a very important part to this success principle that makes it much easier to apply, understand, and integrate into your life. Everything is always happening for you to bring you into your power so you can get clear on what you really want and create your reality the way you want it to be. Everything is always happening for you to bring you into your power, to bring you into truth, into clarity so you can create your life, aligned to your highest truth, the way you intended it to be.

When something occurs in your life—no matter what it is, even if in that moment you can't see how it's happening for you—try to acknowledge that maybe it *is* happening for you. Ask yourself, "Is it possible that this could be in some way happening for me? Could this in some way be helping me realize more of my own personal power instead of a habit of feeling victimized, powerless, or not good enough?"

One student asks, "What if you find it challenging to stay in your power and not feel powerless or victimized in your situation?" The first thing I would suggest is to stop whatever you are doing or thinking for a moment and take three conscious deep breaths. Ask yourself the question, "What am I giving my power away to in this moment?" You could be giving your power away to a belief you have, to someone else, to your circumstances, or unconsciously giving your power away for no reason.

Once you see where you are giving your power away, observe how your situation helped you to realize that you were giving your power away. Begin to imagine that your own personal power is not flowing back to you from whatever you gave your power away to. Then, notice whether there is clarity about what you do want or the reality that you do want to create.

If you can open to that potential, you might discover that almost instantly you are aware of ways that this is happening for you. That's all it takes! Your ability to perceive the situation differently will immediately help you see how this situation is happening for you, not to you.

SEE THE GIFT

I had a dear friend whose husband had been diagnosed with life-threatening cancer and was given up to five years to live. They owned a large home on a large property that required a lot of upkeep, maintenance, and continuous repairs. They built the house themselves and loved it so much they never imagined selling it. However, the home had become quite overwhelming to maintain, especially with her husband's diagnosis and demanding treatment schedule.

Her husband had undergone several surgeries and was about to go in for major surgery to remove the cancer. The doctor had warned them of the likelihood that when they opened him up, they might realize there was nothing they could do and no further surgery would be performed. It was the day prior to the surgery and my friend was stressed, anxious, and fearful.

As I was listening to her share her feelings of overwhelm, I felt guided to ask her a question that almost didn't seem compassionate. However, the nudge to ask kept getting stronger. I said to my friend, "I want to ask you a crazy question. You don't have to answer me, but I feel guided to ask you." And she said, "Go ahead." I said, "Is it possible in some way that this could all be happening for you in some way? Has there been any gift that has come from all of this?" She immediately responded with, "Oh, you're right, that is kind of a crazy question." She paused for several seconds and then she laughed a little, but it kind of took the edge off just a bit. She said, "You know what? In some ways this has been a gift. We have come to the realization that I don't think we ever would have gotten to without all this cancer stuff, that we really need to sell our house and downsize to be prepared for the next chapter of our lives." And she said, "If we hadn't gone through all of this, there's no way we would have ever come to that, and it probably would have gotten rundown and been an issue."

After she acknowledged that, she kept going. She told me about how for the first time ever in years, all her kids and their significant others came home to spend the holidays with them. She said, "We've had conversations about life and the meaning of life that we have never had in thirty-plus years of being together." She said, "I have learned more about health and wellness in this experience than I ever could have imagined." And she said, "So, yeah, there are gifts in this. I can see how this is happening for me. I can see that maybe there's something here that could be a gift."

I could tell she felt much better, and the conversation then changed to other things. She seemed peaceful about the upcoming surgery. At times, it might take a lot of strength to be in a situation like the death of a loved one, a disease, or a diagnosis, either yourself or someone else, a near-death experience, or an injury, and have the courage to see the gift in there somewhere.

Take having an injury, for example. It's not to say you *caused* yourself the injury but is it possible that there's a gift in here somewhere.

I have a friend who is extremely active, active in her career, active in her life, plays a lot of sports, and is always *busy.* This friend is also a highly intuitive channel herself and wanted to start creating offerings and services doing channeling. But she was always so busy with everything else going on that she never had time for it.

One afternoon, she broke her foot. At the time, it seemed terrible and unfortunate. My friend was upset that now she couldn't do all the things that kept her busy and active. However, soon after, she changed her tune. She started commenting on how she was finally going to have the time to slow down, tune in and listen to her soul, and cultivate her gifts, abilities, and services without constantly being distracted. She had a new sense of personal power, clarity, and was excited to create an incredible business that now she loves.

Another student asked a common question: "What if you feel challenged and overwhelmed about how to get your message out in the world?" My response: "Start exactly where you are. Source can deliver someone *in this day* whose life could be transformed by your message, your gift, your story."

START WHERE YOU ARE

I have a longstanding client who, years ago, felt called to write a book. He wanted to inspire people and share his life story in the hope that it would inspire others. He said, "I really want to inspire people, so I am going to write a book, but it's going to take me two or three years before I can write the book, get it published, and start inspiring and empowering people."

In his mind, the only way he would be credible enough to share his message with others was if he wrote a book and was a published author. The Council said, "Find some way *in this day* to share your gift, to share your message, to do what it is that you feel inspired to do without making this a big obstacle. In this day, Source can deliver someone whose entire life could be transformed for the better once they meet you and hear your story!" It could be someone you meet at the coffee shop, grocery store, post office, or out on a walk. And you know what, that exact day, he met his first client and started coaching people while writing his book.

Years ago, I had the dream to be on Oprah's *Super Soul Sunday.* I was in the corporate world. I had not written any books yet, had no platform, no website, no reason at all to think I could ever be on Oprah. Yet I imagined myself sitting under the oak trees in Santa Barbara with Oprah Winfrey talking about spirituality, consciousness, and the wisdom of The Council.

That dream in my heart was inspiring and uplifting to me, but I had no idea how that was ever going to happen. Some years later, I was offering private sessions with The Council, doing courses, and had many students. I hadn't published any books, and I still had the dream to be on Oprah's *Super Soul Sunday.* I happened to live at that time about two miles from Oprah's home. I would sit under my oak trees at my house, imagining that somehow they were connected to Oprah's oak trees. I would imagine that Oprah was asking me questions, interviewing me for her show. I would answer her out loud sitting under my oak trees.

Much to my surprise and *out of the blue* one day, not long after that, I was contacted by someone at Gaia TV. His name was Reuben Langdon, and he had a show on the network called *Interviews with Extra Dimensionals.* He said, "I'd like to come to your home in Santa Barbara and interview you for my show. I'd love to do an episode on you and your life as a channel and another episode where I ask questions to The Council."

Soon after, he and his film crew came to my home, and for three days we filmed two episodes for his television show in the exact location that I imagined myself sitting under the oak trees talking to Oprah. We filmed footage with my dog and my cat, in my home, in my Heaven on Earth. We filmed at the places that I loved, where I went to hike, where I watched the sunset, a temple that I loved visiting—it was truly beyond my wildest dreams. It was even better because it was at *my home*, with my animals, featuring my life and what I enjoyed doing, and I got to share it with the world.

So where do you start? What if you're challenged? Start right where you are. Find some way in this day to begin right where you are. Find some way today to imagine and feel exactly what it is you want to experience. If doubt comes up, keep going or start again tomorrow. Have fun with this and don't create a huge, impossible gap between where you are and the experience you desire to have.

From time to time, students express that they are experiencing feelings of depression and ask what it may mean. People are often feeling as if they are depressed because they're feeling powerless in their life. They feel powerless to create their reality the way they want it to be, and many have felt this way for years. Understandably, that could be very depressing, especially if over a long period of time you don't feel like you have the power or the clarity for what you want to create in your life.

Remember, whatever has brought you to this moment was happening for you. Get clear on your power. Ask yourself, "In what way am I giving my power away?" What are you giving your power to? You might be thinking that you are not powerful enough to have the experience you want to have. And if something happens and you catch yourself questioning, "Why is this happening to me?" stop, take three deep breaths, and ask yourself these questions: "Where am I giving my power away here? Who am I giving my power to? What am I giving my power to? In what way am I placing my own personal power somewhere *out there*?"

Observe yourself (or others) without judgment and discern what you're giving your power to. Maybe you are giving your power to an old story, a limited belief you have, a habit or thought, a political party or person on television, a former or current partner, friend, or family member. Just start to see where you are giving away your power and it will help you get clear on the experience you do want to create in your life.

It might be difficult in certain situations like the death of a loved one to see how it's happening for you. That's okay. Give yourself some time, but consider this: Is it possible in some way, that someday, just maybe there could be a gift in this for you or someone you love?

SHIFT YOUR PERSPECTIVE

Years ago, I heard the story of Nancy Brinker and her sister, Susan G. Komen, who passed away from breast cancer in 1980. Nancy believed Susan's outcome might have been better had she known more about breast cancer signs and early detection. Nancy started Susan G. Komen for the Cure and The Promise Fund to support awareness, prevention, and early detection of breast cancer and now other forms of cancer. It is believed that millions of women's lives, and men's, have been saved because of these foundations and awareness about early detection of breast cancer.

There are examples like this that positively affect millions of lives, and they are the simplest little things. One day, I was driving my car, and I was running a little late. I was probably going a little fast, and I was clearly a little too close to the car in front of me, when all of a sudden, a rock hit my window and chipped my windshield. At first, I was irritated and upset, but then I took some deep breaths and asked, "How is this happening for me?" I heard a voice in my head say, "Slow down."

So, I did, and I started to slow down when I was driving. I started to not drive so close behind other cars because I didn't want to get another ding in my windshield. A couple weeks later, I *was* driving more slowly, I *was* paying a little bit better attention, when the car in front of me slammed on its brakes and came to a dead stop. The car behind me was not really slowing down, but because I wasn't following too close, I could see what was going on behind me, I could see what was happening in front of me, and I was able to check the side and move to the side so that the car behind me didn't hit me or so I didn't rear-end the other car *and* have someone hit me.

As I sat there in my car, I felt chills go through my body. Not because I avoided the car accident, but because I *knew* in that moment the chip in my window was happening for me, not to me, to get clarity on slowing down, not following cars so close, and so in *this moment*, I would avoid what might have been a significant car crash involving myself and others.

These teachings work for the seemingly simple things and the *big things in life*. In any moment, you can shift your perspective of whatever is happening to know that in some way, it's happening for you. You might avoid seriously unwanted circumstances or inspire the world when you begin to find your power, get clarity, and create your life the way you want it to be, while also advocating for early disease detection and cures that could save millions of lives.

If you want to experience anything in the world around you, you must first create it within yourself.

"The first step is always to go within.
If you want to create anything, you must first create it
within yourself. In all circumstances, the first step is always you."

—THE COUNCIL

You are so much more than you know yourself to be. And while you are the magnificent human and magnificent personality that is you, you are so much more. You are the *Isness of All That Is* and will ever be, and the truth of your Divine nature is peace, a peace so powerful, a peace so unwavering that in every moment you know whatever it is, it's perfect, because you know there is a grander perspective, there is more going on here that you can see, and there is more going on here within each of you, bringing you into greater levels of awareness of who you really are.

All things work together in perfect harmony if you will allow them to. And where you perceive a lack of harmony, it is your opportunity to realign with the perfection of All That Is and create within yourself harmony, peace, love, joy, well-being, abundance, freedom, and beauty.

Take a moment right here right now and consciously, intentionally, align to the feeling of peace. Go from your head fully into your heart. Come fully into your beingness. You may notice that it's quiet, it's light, there's a softness, and yet it's powerful, there's a freedom, and yet it's unwavering.

Take some breaths as you fully tune your awareness to the feeling of peace. Because we assure you that in every moment, no matter what is going on in your world or the world around you or with others, you can align to the peace that is within you, your true Divine nature, in any moment. And why is this so important? Because from this place you summon the energy for all potentials and all possibilities.

When you align with harmony by taking some deep conscious breaths, going into your heart, coming into a place of presence in this moment, you are creating harmony in your body, in your force field, in your environment. You're creating harmony in your thoughts, in your emotions. You're creating the feeling of harmony. You are aligning to the vibrational frequency of harmony, which expands the harmony that you experience.

Harmony is powerful. Think about your magnificent body. When you focus on aligning yourself to a place of peace and then to a place of harmony, everything in your body starts to tune to a frequency that is harmonious. Where there was disharmony or dis-ease or imbalance in the body, the body immediately responds to the feeling of harmony and begins to create a harmonious alignment to everything within your physical body. As you powerfully focus into peace and harmony, every cell of your body begins to tune to a more harmonious existence.

If there is misalignment in the body, in that moment, your cells begin to rejuvenate and regenerate more harmoniously. And the more you enjoy consciously, intentionally creating peace and harmony within, the faster your body will regenerate itself and every cell to live in a more peaceful and harmonious state of being.

As you create this within yourself, it begins to move into your extended existence. You are more than just this body, this magnif-icent human, this magnificent personality that you know as you. You are a force field of consciousness made up of particles of infinite creation. You are a vibrational signature who is known throughout all of the Universe.

Your state of being is so much more powerful than you could ever understand, more powerful than we could ever explain. Once you are aligned, a state of peace and harmony within you creates a vibrational force field that is so truly magnificent. We will use the words *more powerful*, but we mean it from a standpoint of more influential to the collective human consciousness than any states of being that are currently in fear or war or chaos or struggle or suffering.

You may never be able to prove that your elevating yourself and creating peace and harmony positively influences the collective human consciousness, but we know with absolute certainty from our viewpoint and our perspective, fully able to see the vibrational signature that is you, we can see your vibration and your frequency moving through the particles of infinite creation, moving through the force field of consciousness, elevating the collective human consciousness, and any and all who are allowing in that moment, to a greater realization of peace within themselves and harmony within themselves. Your impact, your influence, your contribution when you yourself are in a state of peace and harmony, reaches out into the entire collective human consciousness and makes it easier for all who are ready. And so many are.

IF YOU DESIRE PEACE, CREATE PEACE

If you want to experience anything in the world around you, you must first create it within yourself. One of my students explains it beautifully: "I heard it is not you existing in the Universe, it is the Universe existing in you if you will allow it." If you want peace and harmony in the world, but cannot create it within yourself, it will always elude you in the outer world. And you would not even be aware of the desire for peace and harmony if it wasn't already within you.

If you want peace in your world, you must first create peace within yourself. If you are experiencing chaos within yourself, in your thoughts, in your emotions, in the way that you feel, you are not contributing to peace in the world around you in that moment. It all starts within. You must first create it within yourself and that is what you contribute to the collective.

In the moment you have the awareness that you want peace in the world or peace in your life, you are initiating the process of aligning to it and creating the experience of it. The awareness of choosing peace, and that you can choose peace, that moment allows you to start perceiving your own alignment to it. The awareness of something desired allows you to begin to perceive it, and to create the reality of it within yourself. When you create peace within yourself, you begin to send a signal to the outer world of peace, and you begin to draw more and more experiences of peace into your reality.

I recall an interview I did one time where the host asked The Council about how he could stay in a peaceful state when going through something difficult. At the time, he was in a disagreement and legal battle with a former business partner and found it to be very upsetting. He wanted peace in the situation, he wanted peace in his life again, and he wanted peace with this other person. However, all he could focus on was the disharmony, fighting, and feud between them.

It's common when something's going on in someone's life that one tends to focus on what's wrong, whose fault it is, how terrible it is, which often results in feeling powerless to create the peace and harmony one desires in their life. However, the first step is always you. You must first create what you desire within yourself by aligning to it and feeling it within you.

I can think of a time in my life when living with my former partner that things in our home had become very chaotic. I found myself feeling overwhelmed, frustrated, out of balance. It became clear that this situation was happening for me, to help me be clear on what I really wanted, which was peace and harmony in my home, in the relationship, and in my situation. Yet, I was feeling the exact opposite within myself and felt powerless to change it. I quickly realized that you can't feel the exact opposite within yourself of what you want and create it in the world around you in your life.

I practiced becoming conscious of when I felt feelings of disharmony. I would stop and take three or more deep conscious breaths until I felt better. Then, I would go into my heart and imagine what harmony felt like. Before long I would start to feel that harmony within. I would practice this often. It was obvious that I felt better, but I had no idea how it would change my experience. I kept doing the process, and within a couple of months the entire situation changed. I had created around me the same harmony I was experiencing within me.

I want to share with you a powerful process to create within yourself that which you most want to experience in the world around you. When you want to create something in your environment or in the world, start by asking yourself, "What do I really want?" For example, say you are watching the news and seeing war or devastation. Instead of going into feelings of powerlessness, ask yourself, "What do I want for the people in these war-torn countries?" Your answer might be peace. Then close your eyes and take at least three deep, conscious, intentional breaths. Go from your head into your heart. Move your focus and awareness from your head down into your heart. Then ask yourself, "What does peace feel like?" You might reply, "Calm, safe, relaxed, light."

Feel it within yourself. When you feel peace, then focus your awareness on aligning every cell in your body to that feeling of peace from the top of your head to the bottom of your feet, align every cell with that feeling of peace. Stay in the awareness that you are directing the cells from your heart. If it's peace you want to create in the world around you, go into your heart, feel what peace feels like, and then align every cell of your body to that vibration or frequency or feeling of peace.

Once you feel peace in every cell of your body, expand that feeling one foot around you in every direction. Focus your awareness on directing the particles of infinite creation around you to align with that feeling of peace. Then move your awareness to the room that you're in and align every particle of infinite creation in the room that you're in into that feeling of peace.

Now expand that from your heart into the hearts of those that you most desire to feel peace in this moment. You can expand it into the hearts of specific people or intend it for all of humanity. You might imagine peace moving through the particles of infinite creation over the grass and through the trees and into the air and up above, up to the clouds, down into the Earth, and imagine every single particle of infinite creation as far as your awareness can perceive is aligned to that feeling of peace.

If you do this, you might find that you truly can experience the peace within you creating peace in the world around you. You can use this same process to create harmony, love, joy, abundance, freedom, or well-being within yourself and in the world around you. If you want to experience a loving relationship where you feel adored, treasured, cherished, respected, and appreciated, and yet you haven't aligned to your own self-love, self-appreciation, and self-respect, no matter how much someone tries to love you, if you can't align and create love within yourself, you can't receive it from or experience it with those around you.

Your thoughts affect your emotions. Your emotions held over time affect the way that you feel. The way that you feel is determining your vibration. Your vibration is determining your experience of reality or what you're drawing into your life as your reality. If at any point you notice that your reality is not what you want it to be, come back to the powerful process from the previous paragraphs and create within yourself that which you desire to create in the world around you.

You get more of what you are, not what you want.

"You don't get what you want. You don't get what you say you want.
You don't get what you tell your friends you need and want.
You get more of what you are!"

— THE COUNCIL

You can have it all. You can be fully in realization of all that you are *and* in the realization of your soul's desires fully manifested in your physical experience. Infinite intelligence is available to you in every moment, always guiding you, always supporting you, always out ahead of you orchestrating things on your behalf. Your soul's desires, your soul's highest expression in physical form is known throughout all the Universe. Come into *absolute knowing* of the Divine, perfect unfolding. You wait for nothing. You want for nothing. You lack *nothing*. You are powerful. You are Creator. You are a realized master. *Let it all in. Let it all come to you.*

When you are in the moment of your most glorious manifestation presenting itself to you, take one more breath, savor this moment, expand this moment, and truly receive all that is here for you, because there is so much even beyond the physical manifestation that is available to you in the moment, and while you will fully, completely enjoy your glorious manifestation, it is the *feeling* that you truly desire most. It is *feeling* excited. It is *feeling* expansive. It is *feeling* free. It is *feeling*. It is the *feeling* of love. It is the *feeling* of abundance. It is the *feeling* that really is the best part.

And you can feel it now. And you can feel it in the moment of the glorious manifestation. And you can feel it forevermore, happily ever after, because you know *the manifestation is fun, creation is exciting, but it's all about the feeling,* the feeling of excitement, the feeling. It's all about the feeling.

As you observe the emotions that are present, from time to time you will say, "Well, I don't always feel joyful or happy." But, if it is your choosing, happily ever after is not a place you go, it's not a thing you get. It's a state of consciousness that *is* truly available to you in every moment.

You might say, "Well, sometimes I feel awful. When I do feel happy, it just feels that much better. I need the days and the moments of feeling awful so that the moments of feeling joyful are obvious to me." You are Creator. You get to choose.

You might also be aware that living in a state of being where absolutely *nothing* could make you *any* happier than you are right now is the feeling most closely aligned to the truth of who you really are. Feeling unworthy is not the truth of you. Feeling angry is not the truth of you. Feeling depressed is not the truth of you. Feeling alone is far from the truth of you. Being so satiated, in your power, in the moment, so filled up with all of you—the love that you are, the light that you are, and all that is here for you *now*—as the consciousness and the energy that is in *everything* is your natural state of being.

As you feel into this place, begin to move your awareness. Understand that *absolutely nothing could make me any happier than I am right now.* That is your reality. Imagine saying to yourself, "This is where I am, this is who I am, this is what I am. I am the absolute knowing that absolutely nothing could make me any happier than I am right now."

You have already shifted your awareness and your perspective upon this potential that is a reality that already exists here for you, if it is your choosing. The more you are in that state of *absolutely nothing could make me any happier than I am right now* you continue to experience more happiness and more happiness, and even more satiated feelings of being happy, and even more things to be happy about, and even more happiness in the world and the experiences around you.

YOU GET MORE OF WHAT YOU *ARE*

You get more of what you *are*, not what you want or think you need. The more you allow the happiness that is the natural state of you, the more happiness you draw to you, the more happiness is reflected to you in your reality and all around you, the more things there are to be happy about. *It is* a state of being that you can *choose*, just like you can choose to be frustrated, just like you can choose to focus your thoughts upon your unworthiness, just like you can choose to focus your thoughts upon your lack, just like you can choose to focus upon the unknown and fear the future. Or you can focus on the unknown and get so excited because you know infinite intelligence is always available to you. Your soul's desires and the highest expression of your soul in physical form is known throughout the entire Universe, *absolute knowing* that it's all being orchestrated for you.

You are Creator of your reality. You do create reality, and simultaneously, it is created for you. You are the observer, the one who realizes, the one who witnesses, the one who enlightens, and you are the one who created it all. You get to experience God while also being God. You get to experience creation while also being Creator and the consciousness and the energy that created it all.

This is an invitation to go beyond needing and wanting to align with your Divine nature and your higher self in this moment. When you start to think of getting more of what you are, not what you want or think you need, you elevate yourself beyond limitation to align to your highest potential and all that you are.

When you say, "I want it because I don't have it, I need it because I don't have it," you are in lack and limitation, which will always create separation from that very thing you say you want or need. You get more of what you are, not what you want. If you want more joy in your life, align to the joy that is already within you and around you.

It's common to think or say, "Oh, I need that," or "I want that," don't judge yourself. Just be aware. You simply cannot be in lack of money and aligned to your abundance. You cannot be focused on your ill health and aligned to your well-being. You cannot be in separation and aligned to your connection to Source Energy. Focus on what you do have and what you want to create more of in your life.

ALIGNING WITH WHAT YOU HAVE

Some years ago, one of my students illustrated this principle so well. She was approaching retirement age and in fear that she wouldn't have money to live on the rest of her life. She talked about it openly and continually focused on her lack of money and how limited her options were now that she was approaching retirement. She would go on to say that she was not married and had no one to support her. However, when asked what she wanted, she would say, "I need money."

Some months later, a family member who was quite young died unexpectedly and had left her a large inheritance. She was sad for the loss of her beloved family member and yet, so relieved and excited to receive the money she inherited. Not long after receiving her inheritance, paying off her bills and debts, and putting the remainder in savings, the same fear overcame her except now it wasn't that she didn't have any money for retirement, it was, "Oh my God, what if I lose all this money somehow?" Now, the attention she used to have on not having money for retirement was transferred into the fear of losing the money.

Another student explains that, prior to understanding this principle, she had been focused on and perceiving only a lack of well-being in her body over a long period of time. She started to focus on all the things in her body that *are* already aligned to well-being. Almost instantly, she started to experience more and more well-being. Now she says she feels better than she has in years! She is realizing even more of the well-being that was already within.

If you want more joy in your life, align with the joy that is already within you and all around you. If you want to experience more abundance in your life, then become the most abundant person you know. If you want to experience more well-being, notice all the ways that you have well-being. You don't get what you want or think you need; you get more of what *you are.*

You can shift your perspective at any time to see how abundant you are, how much well-being you have, how much love that you do have, the gifts and abilities that you do have. I often hear students say, "I don't know what my gifts are. I don't know what my purpose is." They are so focused on *I don't know*. They truly can't see their amazing gifts and live their purpose when they are perceiving and believing that they don't know. You get more of what you *are*.

A woman in our community said to The Council while asking a question, "I have just known all my life that I was going to be a wealthy woman." Then she went on to tell the story about how she was struggling with money, how she was afraid to lose her house, how she had no idea how she was going to pay her bills, and most importantly, how incredibly worried her family and children were about her financial situation. She said, "My family is so worried about me. My kids are so worried about me going broke. But I have always felt like I was supposed to be or that I was going to be a wealthy woman."

You can easily tell the signal that you are sending to the Universe by what is being reflected back to you. How does this person's family and children know that she's struggling with money? Because that's what she's talking about, that's what she's focused on, that's what she's telling them: how broke she is, how much lack she's experiencing, how scared she is that she can't pay her bills. She's not feeling or aligning to the abundance that she does have or the wealth she believes she is destined to have.

Have you noticed on your cell phone that when you mention something like vacationing in a certain place or buying a certain product, some form of intelligence seems to hear you, and the next time you get online, there are ads for the very place you desire to vacation or product you want to buy. Or maybe you've searched for something online like buying a new suitcase, and then suddenly, your social media platforms show you deals on luggage. Technology is reflecting to you that someone or something is getting the message you are broadcasting and it's reflecting to you what you're focused on. The Universe works the same way. It hears what you say and knows what you are focused on.

The same is true in what other people around you are reflecting back to you about what you are focused on. What others reflect back to you is showing you precisely what message the Universe is getting from you. If you know you are a wealthy person, then start affirming that you are abundant, prosperous, and wealthy. Start talking about the ways you are abundant and start using the word *wealthy* in ways that feel true to you. For example, you might say, "I have amassed a wealth of knowledge and experience in my life. I feel like the wealthiest person in the world to have such a wonderful, caring family." Or you might say, "I am wealthy. I am wealthy. I am wealthy."

Why do you want wealth? What would your life be like if you were wealthy? What does it feel like to *be* wealthy? Your answer might be *freedom*. It might offer you the freedom to do what you want to do when you want to do it. The freedom to have everything you need when you need it and more. Wealthy might mean to have everything you need and more; to have the resources, the opportunities, the money, the time, the freedom to create and live your life the way you want.

The Council suggested that this student affirm one thing in her mind as she went throughout her day: "I am a wise, wealthy woman, I am a wise, wealthy woman, I am a wise, wealthy woman." You can adapt this to what feels right to you. This woman knew she was very *wise*, so to use the word "wise" felt true and empowering to her.

When The Council offered this exercise, I tried it myself and affirmed each day, "I'm a wise, wealthy woman." Within a few days, someone said to me, "You are such a wise, wealthy woman." I knew this person was going to say it as the words came out of her mouth and I got chills from head to toe. I realized in that moment that I had experienced the *knowing* that the thoughts I am thinking about myself are not just in *my head*, they are being broadcast in a force field of consciousness all around me. What are people around you reflecting back to you? Because that is the very message that the Universe is getting too.

Recently, The Council has been inviting students into a state of *absolutely nothing could make me any happier than I am right now*. Take a moment, practicing this statement out loud and repeat it three times, *"Absolutely nothing could make me happier than I am right now, absolutely nothing could make me more worthy than I am right now, and absolutely nothing could make me feel more abundant than I am right now."*

At first, your brain might say, "Oh, but if I had that, I'd be happier. Oh, if I had this, I'd be happier." Don't judge your thoughts.

Keep affirming and see if you arrive at a place of feeling happier in the moment. Your next thought mind be, "Well, if I affirm to the Universe that I'm *already* happy, the Universe isn't going to give me that thing I want to be happy about." That's just not how it works. You get more of what you *are*, not what you think you need from something outside of you.

You might notice that when you focus on feeling into that place of absolutely nothing could make me any happier, all sorts of things start showing up in your life, and now you're *even* happier, and noticing that your happiness is expanding. It's the state of being you're aligned to in *this* moment, which is how you are creating your reality. It's not about an attachment to material things.

I had a good friend who was going through a very challenging financial time in his life, and he had one asset left to his name. It happened to be his Range Rover. And he refused, completely refused, to sell his Range Rover and get a cheaper car, because he *knew* he was successful, he *knew* he was wealthy, he knew that his car was the energy of who he really was, not the things that were happening at that time.

He went through a difficult divorce and had accumulated large unexpected legal expenses. It was also a time when the economy was slow for his business, and he was struggling to make any profit. He knew that his debts, financial struggles, and business challenges were not who he was. And he refused to sell the one and only asset he had left because when he got in that car it reminded him that he was successful, that he was thriving, even though everything around him seemed to show him that he was broke, struggling, and had failed.

I learned from my friend, watching how he navigated through this experience. It wasn't that he was attached to a car. It was a knowing that that car was a representation of the truth of his abundance and a reminder to him that he would come back from this experience stronger, clearer, and better from the wisdom he gained. He stayed positive and upbeat regardless of the struggles he was facing or amount of money in his bank account. Within one year, he grew his business, paid off his debts, saved some money, and then he bought a new Range Rover! It's not about an attachment to material things. One of my students explains it well. She says, "It's realizing that how I *feel* is what I *am* in the moment."

It's common to think, "I'll be happy *when* I have a certain amount of money. I'll be able to create what I want to create. I'll be able to do what I want to do. I'll be able to have what I want to have." When a student is feeling this way, The Council might say, "Alright, what's the amount of money? What's the amount of money you want to have so that you will *finally* be happy and be free, and have the money to do the things you want to do?"

One student responded and said, "One million dollars." The Council said, "Anytime you want to buy something, do something, have something, go somewhere, first, feel, and align to the feeling that you have that million dollars right now. Go within and imagine that you do have that money *now*. Not *if* I had one million dollars but go to the feeling of *having it* now. How does that *feel*? What does that feel like?" It's about the feeling that you will have when you have the thing you want to have and aligning to it right here, right now.

YOUR IMAGINATION HAS POWER

When you feel into what you want right now without resistance because you don't have it, you are aligning to the reality you want to create. Play in your imagination. Have fun *feeling* your way into the experience that you desire.

The Council talks about the 3rd Dimension, the 4th Dimension, the 5th Dimension, and the 6th Dimension. The 6th Dimension is where it's *all* here for you now. In your imagination, you can be anywhere, at any moment, having the experience you desire *now*! Imagine being in a rowboat on a beautiful, calm lake, under the stars, floating on the water, looking out at the moonlight glistening on the waves. Can you see it in your imagination and feel yourself there?

You can go anywhere in your imagination right now and feel as if you are there! You don't need to drag the rowboat down the shore to the water. You don't need to drive to the lake. And notice, although it's nighttime in your imagination, you're not tired.

The 6th Dimension is the realm of pure potential and imagination, where everything is available to you. You are separate from nothing. There is no limitation. There is no delay. The 6th Dimension is a *reality,* it's real. It's the realm of imagination, the realm of pure potential.

You might imagine that you're out fishing with your grandfather, whom you loved so much, at his favorite fishing spot. He made the perfect lunch, those special sandwiches that he always made, and little Snickers bars, with a soda pop. You and your grandfather are out on the lake on a beautiful, crisp, quiet, day fishing, catching fish after fish, then throwing them back into the water. You're looking out and watching the fish play in the waves with your beloved grandfather, having the perfect lunchtime snack that was always your favorite as a kid.

Whether you experienced this with your grandfather or not, if you will allow yourself into your imagination, *you're there.* If you don't deny yourself that experience because it's not *real,* you can literally focus yourself into any experience through your feeling and imagination.

That's not to say you're not in the *present moment.* You are focusing yourself into a dimension of consciousness that is available to you in *this moment.* You're not denying the present moment and *what is.* When you accept the present moment just as it is, you can play and create from a state of knowing who you already are. You get more of what you are, not what you want. If you want more of anything in your life, align to the feeling of it and the reality of it that is already within you!

When you are resisting anything, you are resisting everything.

"In letting go, you let it all in. In letting go, you let it all in. When you resist anything, you resist everything. When you allow one thing in, you allow everything in. When you allow your joy, when you allow your happiness, when you allow your well-being, when you allow your abundance, you allow everything. Love comes out of the blue. Prosperity, freedom, beauty, it's all there, and there's nothing missing and nothing left out. It's all there. It's all here."

— THE COUNCIL

The creative process is so powerful. The creative process is life itself. The creative process is evident in all that exists in all life forms. When you are not intentionally focused on the creative process, you tend to feel disconnected from the manifestation that you would like to experience. Life isn't that exciting. There isn't the momentum you wish to have. You're not experiencing the magic and the miracles because you're not allowing yourself into the creative process where everything is here, now, for you to receive and for you to celebrate.

Create, create, create, dear master, for the fun of creating, for the joy of creating, for the magic of creating, for the power of creating. If you make a salad or a sandwich or are cooking a delicious meal, you are creating. You are creating a masterpiece if it is your perspective, if it is your focus. When you are writing a letter, you are creating. When you are typing a message, you are creating. When you are preparing your body for the day with your clothing and your hair and your style, you are creating.

When you begin to play in the creative process all throughout the day, you find that life becomes more fun, life becomes more enjoyable, life becomes more beautiful. You feel more passionate, you feel more inspiration, you're more tuned in to intuition, and the energy that is lighting the way is brighter. The energy flows and there is more clarity. But you must be in the creative process.

Consciousness moves energy into form. And when you're playing and creating in the consciousness field and summoning energy, you are creating new experiences, new forms, new potentials, and new possibilities. And you're here in this magnificent human experience for the purpose of creating with all that is here because it is all here for you.

You don't have to create the planet. You don't have to create nature. You don't have to create the humans. You don't have to create the cells in your body. You get to play with all that has been created for you, by you, through the consciousness and intelligence and the energy that creates everything. But that consciousness and that intelligence and that energy that created everything, put it all here in form for you to play and to create with and to have fun with and to explore with and to expand with and to express with and to have experiences with.

OPEN, ALLOW, AND RECEIVE

If you're waiting for something, you're missing all that is already here for you. If you're pushing and efforting, you're not allowing and receiving. If you're trying to figure it out, you're certainly not in the energy of celebrating all that is *here now*, all that is *now here*. If you are trying to figure it out, you're not celebrating all that is *here now*.

How do you do this? Focus on joy. Focus on love. Focus on playing. Focus on creating. Focus on having fun. It matters not what you choose to create. It matters that you create with all that is here for you.

Do you have to create a new planet? No. Do you have to create the trees? Do you have to create the sun and the moon and the stars?

No. Do you have to create the animals? No. It's all here for you. Everything is here for you. Everything is here for you now. You will feel so good when you allow yourself to play and create with all that is here for you now.

It matters not what you create, but it does matter the resistance and the expectation you place on your creations. It matters not what you create, but when you put expectations and resistance into your creations from a place of lack, limitation, or separation, you don't fully allow the power of the creative process because you're not open to receiving and you're not in the energy of celebrating all that you have created and all that is here for you.

True Creation has no agenda. Now, you may want to create something from a wonderful place, of wanting to enjoy something's beauty. You may cut beautiful roses from the garden, place them in a vase, because you so love their beauty and enjoy them. But there is an innocence in that. There is a joy in that. There is a fulfillment inherent in the very process of creating and playing and having fun.

Now, if you assign an expectation on it—I have to go sell these roses in order to get what I want because I don't *have* what I want; I'm in the lack of what I want, I am separate from what I want—then there's resistance. If you're creating art, you may think: *I created it, so now it should be the most expensive piece of art ever sold.*

So much of the creative process has become so limited by the expectation and resistance that you place upon that which you have created when the very process itself of creating *is* the important part, the enjoyment of what you have created, the fun in creating it, the innocence in creating it because it makes you happy, because you experience and expand the beauty around you, and it's fun. Let it be fun.

When you are initiating or activating the creative process, you are opening the fields of consciousness that summon the energy for all sorts of manifestations to move into form—most of all are already in form. Are you allowing? Are you receiving? Are you celebrating the *now here*? Are you in an energy of *absolutely nothing could make me any happier than I am right now*?

You want to talk about a powerful point of allowing, receiving, welcoming, and celebrating such that all that you are and all that you have just continues to expand? Do you want to talk about creating a powerful portal for new levels of manifestation and magic and miracles to flow into your life? *It is the energy of absolutely nothing could make me any happier than I am right now.*

You create a powerful portal for expansion, for receiving, for more to flow into your experience, for new and expanded levels of more creating, more creating. You think there is this one thing you want, and once you have it, you'll be happy. This thing that if it would just change and it would be this way, then I would be happy. When this thing comes in, this big thing that's so important to me, then I'll be happy. And yet you do not realize that's not congruent with a space that is open and receiving and allowing, and certainly not the space of celebrating all that is *now here.*

And yet we say when you get into the space of *absolutely nothing could make me any happier than I am right now*, oh, that is where you receive. That is the energy that welcomes in all sorts of new potentials, new possibilities, all sorts of manifestations and examples of True Creation.

Now, yes, you get to create your reality the way you want it to be. But you never have to make yourself miserable and take massive, determined action to the point of exhaustion to get that thing that you want. That is how much of your collective gets what it thinks it wants, and most all of that is based on lack, limitation, and separation. And yet we have said all along to come into a place of pure love, where your well-being and abundance are assured, where you have gone beyond unworthiness and doubt and fear into absolute knowing and then into the absolute knowing that it's *now here* and has been all along, and all that's left to do is receive and allow and celebrate and welcome in all that has been here for you, all that is here.

SURRENDER TO WHERE YOU ARE NOW

Let go, let go of the resistance, of the pushing and the forcing and the efforting. Surrender into creativity. Surrender to the joy of creating. Surrender into the love of what you love. Surrender into the place where *absolutely nothing would make you any happier than you are right now* and be *now here*.

Your words are powerful. There's a big difference between it's *now here* and I've been waiting and trying for so long and so focused on it and making it happen. It's all I think about and all I want and all I could ever want and if it would just come, then I wouldn't ever have to want for anything again. And it hasn't come, and I've thought about it for so long, and I've been trying to make it happen.

In letting go, you let it all in. In letting go, you let it *all* in. When you resist anything, you resist everything. When you allow one thing in, you allow everything in. When you allow your joy, when you allow your happiness, when you allow your well-being, when you allow your abundance, you allow everything. Love comes out of the blue. Prosperity, freedom, beauty, it's all there, and there's nothing missing and nothing left out. It's all there. It's all here.

You are here to create, to play, to have fun, to do the things you love and do the things that bring you joy. You are here to expand into all you are, even though you're everything you wish to be. You are here to express all that you are, the God that you are in physical form. You are here to choose the experiences you want to have for you. You are here to create your reality the way you want it to be. Yes, there is some greater part of you—call it your soul, your spirit, your higher self—that never forgets that you chose to come to this Earth experience at this time for realization. There's nothing more important to your soul than to fully self-realize in physical form, because if you skip that step, if you skip that step, you miss the very best part, which is allowing the highest expression of your soul's desires to manifest in physical form.

The part of you that's never known lack, the part of you that's never known limitation, the part of you that's never known unworthiness, the part of you that has never doubted, and the part of you who has never feared anything, knows your highest expression, knows the dreams in your heart. It knows the manifestation of your soul's desires in physical form, the ones that will surprise you and delight you beyond anything that the limited part of you could ever even think to ask for or dream of or wish for, the highest expression of your soul's desires in physical form for your enjoyment, for the expansion of your creative expression and mastery, for the expansion of all potentials and possibilities.

There is realization, the fully integrated realization of all that you are into your truth, into your wholeness, into your perfection, into your brilliance, into your magnificence, so that everything in your life can reflect back to you that wholeness, that completeness, that perfection, that brilliance, that magnificence of all that you truly are. Receive, receive, receive. Welcome in every part of you. Celebrate every part of you. Welcome in all that is here for you. Celebrate the *now here*. Celebrate all that is here, all that is now. Allow, allow, allow yourself into the place, into the space, into the *absolute knowing that nothing would make you any happier than you are right now*.

Will you have those things that your brain is responding with, that says, well, that would make me happier, well, if this thing changed, it'd make me happier, well, if I had that thing over here? You'll have those things in the moment that you can allow them. Not because you forced and efforted and figured them out and pushed and suffered and struggled and created the resistance and the expectation and the push and the force and the struggle, but because you allowed them, because you allowed yourself to receive them, because you welcomed them, because you celebrated them, because you know it's all *now here*.

And is there a greater intelligence that is divinely orchestrating it all? Absolutely. Do you have free will to choose? Absolutely. Are you a powerful Creator? Absolutely. But you just simply can't get there, not here, not now, not in this level of consciousness, not from this level of awareness, by creating the lack of it and playing a game with yourself of forcing and struggling and efforting your way to it. You can't play in old levels of consciousness, in the old energy and expect the new.

You want something new. We said absolutely nothing could make you any happier than you are right now, to which your brain said, no, there is this thing. But you want to go into the old energy, in the old consciousness, and push and force and effort it, and you cannot go into the old to receive the new. You come into the new and realize it's been there all along. It is *now*, and it's *here,* and it's *now here.*

LET GO OF RESISTANCE

When you are resisting anything, you are resisting everything. Now, here's the good news, the opposite is also true. When you start to focus on allowing anything in your life, you open up and start allowing everything. *Everything.*

Resistance creates tension, constriction, stress, and limits the flow of energy. You might easily be able to notice what resistance feels like in the body. To notice what resistance feels like, tightly form a fist in your hand and squeeze as tightly as you can. Hold it for approximately five seconds and then let go. Then, open your hand, stretch your fingers. Notice the difference between contraction, which is resistance, and expansion.

Resistance often makes people feel stuck, blocked, you feel overwhelmed, uncertain, or stressed. In fact, stress is a result of resistance. When you are holding yourself in resistance, you're slowing your vibrational frequency, lowering your consciousness, and as a result, focusing yourself into lack, limitation, fear, and separation. When you lower your consciousness and slow your vibration, you create resistance in your body. You might also notice when you are unconsciously creating resistance, when you are holding your breath, clenching your hands or teeth, slumping in your chair, or hunching over.

You might be feeling resistance about how someone's treating you in your relationship. However, in that moment you are also resisting your own well-being, the flow of love, your own love, your worthiness, and your peace and harmony. When you resist anything at all, you're resisting everything.

You can begin to understand that by looking at three areas of one's life: work and finances, relationships and love, and health and body. A person who is going through a challenging financial time and struggling with money might describe feeling stressed, overwhelmed, fearful, or worried. These feelings create resistance and constrict energy flow in the body. They might also notice that they are easily triggered or angered in their relationships.

Think about when you have something going on in your body, such as pain or sickness. It affects your relationships and ability to work. One might also experience this when going through a breakup.

The emotional resistance one feels can affect one's work and lead to sickness in the body.

When you're feeling or experiencing resistance in any area of your life, it creates stress and overwhelm that affects all other areas of your life. It constricts the energy like a kink in a garden hose constricts the water flow. Think of water flowing through a hose like your flow of abundance, well-being, and love. When you stop the water flowing through the hose, you are stopping the flow of energy that attracts abundance, well-being, and love. When you're resisting anything, you're resisting everything and stopping the flow of easy, effortless, harmonious creation. However, when you allow anything, you allow everything.

How do you know if you're in a state of *allowing*? The instant manifestation of allowing is *joy*. The most powerful state you can be in for easy, effortless, harmonious creation is feeling joyful, feeling joy in your body, in your life, in your relationships, in your finances, in your work. When you are feeling joyful, focusing on what brings you joy, and doing the things that bring you joy, you open yourself up to everything good flowing into your life easily, effortlessly, and harmoniously.

Your thoughts affect your emotions, your emotions affect the way you feel, your feelings determine whether you feel resistance or expansion. If you feel resistance, notice your thoughts. If you are thinking thoughts such as, I'm not smart enough, I'm not good enough, I'm *supposed* to be doing this or that, I can't do that, I'm not loved or not worthy, you can feel yourself contract or constrict. When you are thinking thoughts that feel good, you will feel open and free. Are you feeling a constriction of energy, or do you feel expansive, like anything is possible?

When you do the things that bring you joy, you feel alive. You feel lighthearted. You feel like a sense of being *in the flow*. Things come together for you. Things are easy, effortless, harmonious when you're in that state of joy. The instant manifestation of allowing is *joy*. You will know that you're in a state of allowing when you feel joy.

You can't be in joy and hold yourself in resistance. If you are feeling resistance, come back into the moment and take some deep, conscious, intentional breaths, and go from your head to your heart. Feel yourself expanding. You can feel expansion on your inhale, and you can also feel expansion on the exhale. Take deep, conscious, intentional breaths, and you can easily shift into greater ease and into flow of creation.

Channeled Activation for Experiencing Your Life

We are so pleased and delighted to have the opportunity to speak with you on this fine and glorious day indeed. We remind you that while our words to you are important, this is a vibrational experience, an activation of remembering the truth within you, the power within you, and your intention for this life experience to be everything you desire it to be for your intention of joy and fun, expansion, play, creativity as you integrate every part of you into your wholeness, your fullness, your completion, dear beloved.

Your innocence is your power. Your creativity, your playfulness, your joyfulness is your power. You are here to create your life and everything you intend it to be. We come forth because we promised we would so that you do not lose your way in the envisioning of your life the way you choose it to be, the creating of your life the way you choose it to be, and the experiencing of your magnificent life the way you choose it to be.

You are experiencing life through your physical senses, what you see, what you hear, what you taste, what you touch, what you smell, and what you think, and you are the one choosing the experience. Your perception—your perspective—is determining your experience of life.

We wish to remind you that anything and everything, dear master, is possible for you. When you come into this moment, into your power, and you expand it into Oneness with all that is throughout all of creation, you allow the particles of infinite, infinite, infinite creation that are always responding to you to reflect to you the experience of the most abundant, joyful, peaceful, glorious life.

We know not all times are easy. We know there are times when you can feel that change is under way, transformation is occurring, something new is in the process of presenting itself to you. This is time to celebrate, to appreciate, and to welcome in the expansion and an enhanced experience of life and all that is possible for you.

Everything is here for you. You are here to experience life itself. You are here to experience yourself as life. You are here to experience life itself, and you are here to experience yourself as life. It can be as grand and magnificent as you are willing to allow it. Give permission for the particles of infinite creation to efficiently and expeditiously and gracefully present to you an experience of life, an experience of yourself as life beyond what you have ever allowed before. You are ready. You are prepared. It is time. Oh, you have drawn this all to you. You are a master. You are a master because you have chosen to be. It is all here for you now.

As you have integrated and applied this wisdom to come fully into realization of self, you allow the grand, magnificent experience of all of life in all its glory to be presented to you, to be realized by you, to be enjoyed by you.

Have fun. Have fun. Have fun. Cherish the moments of joy. Celebrate the creation and your creativity. Allow your abundance and well-being. Allow love to always lead the way. Let the next perfect step come to you.

You are everything you wish to be. You already are. It is all within you. It always will be. And we are always here for you, always with you, always available to you.

This is just the beginning of so much more as you come into absolute integration, into Oneness, expanding into the stillness, to fully receive the acceleration, the manifestation, the transformation, the realization of all that it is here and possible for you.

We love you, we love you, we love you, and we continue on this magnificent journey with you. But for now, we are complete.

Review: Experiencing Your Life

SUCCESS PRINCIPLE #5: Everything is always happening for you, not to you.

- It is happening *for* you to bring you into your power, so that you can get clear on what you really want and create your reality the way you desire it to be.

- Ask yourself, "What am I giving my power away to in this situation?"

SUCCESS PRINCIPLE #6: If you want to experience anything in the world around you, you must first create it within yourself.

- Go from your head into your heart and align with what you want. Feel it within you in every cell of your body.

- Awareness allows you to perceive it within and draw the experience to you as your reality.

SUCCESS PRINCIPLE #7: You get more of what you are, not what you want.

- If you want more joy in your life, align with the joy that is already within you and all around you.

- Need automatically moves you into a feeling of lack and limitation.

SUCCESS PRINCIPLE #8: When you are resisting anything, you are resisting everything.

- Resistance in any area of your life creates resistance in other areas.

- When you allow anything through your joy, you open up and begin to allow things to flow to you in all areas of your life.

PART III

EXPLORING YOUR CREATION

"There is nothing more important that you will ever do than realize the master that you are of your own human experience, to come into full realization of all that you are, the power that you have, and the Creator that you are within your own creation. You have chosen to know yourself as the master that you are on this magnificent Earth, in this magnificent thing you call life, on this grand adventure at this time. You are the very consciousness and energy that creates everything. You are that consciousness, you are that energy, and therefore you are that which you call God, Source, the Divine. You are that. And yet you're having a journey, a grand adventure of exploring realms of potential and possibility for the pure joy of creating your experience. You get to choose."

— THE COUNCIL

In Part Three, we are exploring creation and the success principles that help you to access your power to create your reality. The Council tells us that we are Creator within our own creation of reality. This includes the reality we create in our minds and the life we create as our reality.

You can begin to explore creation and how you create your reality starting with three main pillars, or playgrounds, as The Council refers to them. These playgrounds for creating your reality include: your health and well-being, your money and abundance, and your relationships.

Let's begin with health and well-being. One of my students asked, "I am affirming and imagining a reality where I feel complete well-being. However, I feel periodic pain in my back and knee. Is that resistance when I can't help being aware of the pain?"

Whenever you are feeling any sort of pain in the body or what you might refer to as resistance in the body, first off, don't judge it and don't judge yourself. Louise Hay offers a wonderful awareness in her book *Heal Your Body* that allows readers to discover when they might be experiencing certain symptoms and how to transform your emotional state to create your physical experience of well-being. Your body is intelligent.

Oftentimes when you experience some sort of disharmony in the body, it is a message from your body. It's a loving message from the body, it's an opportunity to tune in to your body. But don't go into judgment of yourself for doing something wrong or feeling something wrong. What creates resistance when you feel pain comes from when fear and judgment is present, and you push against what is. Instead, align to the reality of well-being that is available to you, even if you are experiencing a sensation of pain in the body.

You can observe the sensation. You can be present as you feel pain. You can be conscious that well-being is available to you. You can be aware of your ability to create the reality you desire to experience without being in judgment of what's going on with your body.

Consider if you had a loved one or someone you care for in your life who was having some sort of pain. Most people would be very compassionate, very loving, very helpful, very supportive to that person they love who is experiencing pain. When someone in your life is experiencing pain or sickness, a typical response would be, "What can I do for you? How can I support you? What would help you to feel better?" To nurture someone you care about, you might sit with them, or put your arms around them, and say, "It's going to be okay." And yet, sometimes people don't give themselves and their own bodies this same level of compassion and care.

YOUR BODY CARRIES A MESSAGE

The first step to creating a reality of well-being when experiencing pain is to stay in a place of nonjudgment, and preferably in a state of compassion for yourself and your body. You can observe what you're feeling. You can also see it as an opportunity to create a space of balance and harmony for your body and a connection to your body. You might find a conscious moment of stillness, knowing that, if there's some sort of message your body has for you, you can tune in to that message in the moment. You can even ask your body if there's a message about this sensation you are feeling that your body would really like you to receive.

To initiate a message from your body, simply place your hand on your heart and close your eyes. Take three deep breaths and move your awareness inward to completely connect with your body. Then, either out loud or in your head, ask your body, "Do you have a message for me? How can I support you in feeling harmony and well-being? Please, body, tell me how I can love and support you. I am open. I love you, body. I'm willing and open to receive your message or guidance." You don't have to recite these exact words. You can refer to this section and use these words for guidance or allow the perfect words that come to you in the moment.

The answer might come immediately, or it might come in the minutes, hours, or days to come. Stay open to receiving communication from your body and know that this connection is supporting you in creating a reality of well-being.

When you are experiencing something in the body that you have commonly referred to as pain, ask yourself, "Are you willing to see it as a *sensation* instead of instantly classifying it as pain?" If you are willing to see it as a sensation, you might feel a greater sense of curiosity about the sensation and how it's your body's way of communicating to you. I'm experiencing a sensation in my body. If you just feel into the difference between the words *pain* versus feeling a *sensation,* you can more easily stay conscious and present instead of going into resistance.

There is a curiosity about it when you are willing to look at it as a sensation in your body. This curiosity allows you to stay open instead of going into a place of resistance because it's *physical pain* that is happening to you. And in your curiosity, you can stay more open to receive a message from your body. You can stay more open to being in a state of compassion. You might notice that the sensation tends to pass more quickly or the awareness that is coming through as a message about that sensation comes through more quickly.

In full disclosure, when The Council first brought this message through in a channel about creating a reality of well-being, my first thought was, "Well, *that's* not going to work!" However, the next time I had a *pain* in my body, I practiced this guidance to see it as a *sensation.* I noticed almost instantly that I was in a peaceful place and felt very present despite the sensation. I placed my hand on my heart and closed my eyes. Immediately, I heard my body say, "Slow down." I kept my hand on my heart and imagined my whole body slowing down and coming into harmony and ease. Within a few minutes, the sensation passed, and I felt a deep sense of gratitude for my body. The result was a knowing that I could create a reality of well-being.

RELEASING LEARNED LIMITATIONS

Another student asks how to release a deep-rooted belief so that we can create our reality the way we desire and explore creation without learned limitations. Referring to any one of the success principles shared in this book will offer you an opportunity to come into a new level of awareness, a new perspective, and to explore not only what's coming up for you, without judgment, but to use the success principles to create a habit or a way of thinking or a perspective that allows you to release that deep-rooted belief, whatever it is.

When a deep-rooted belief comes into your awareness, begin by simply observing it. You can observe a thought, a belief, or an old story without entangling with it. You might begin by writing down the deep-rooted belief. Then, write down the exact opposite statement of that belief. For example, the deep-rooted belief might be, "Anytime something good happens, it doesn't last." What would be the exact opposite of that belief? You might say, "My happiness, joy, abundance, and well-being are always expanding. Everything is always working out *for* me and happening *for* me." Another example might be, "It sucks to get old." The opposite belief would be, "With age comes wisdom, experience, a greater sense of self-worth and self-love. I am getting better and better or becoming happier, healthier, and more peaceful as I age."

Play with it. See how many beliefs you can come up with or statements you can come up with that are exactly the opposite of the belief that you want to release or let go of. Another way to explore this exercise is to write down the belief on one sheet of paper. Then, on a separate sheet of paper, come up with as many things as possible that are exactly the opposite of the deep-rooted belief.

Another common example, "You have to work hard and sacrifice to make money." On a separate piece of paper, write down or say out loud, "Money comes to me easily, effortlessly, and harmoniously. There are so many ways that Source can deliver money to me. I love the energetic exchange of money to receive for all that I am. I love money, and money loves me. Money flows in new and exciting ways. Money flows with effortless ease." Come up with as many things as you can that are the opposite of that belief you want to let go of and start to focus on those things. Play with it until you feel the lightness, playfulness, and fun on creating beliefs that feel good to you. When you are ready, you might discard the sheet of paper with the old belief and continue to affirm the beliefs that support the reality that you want to create.

It's important to be aware that at first your mind might create thoughts of doubt. You might not have ever experienced a reality like the one that you want to create—that's normal and natural. Continue to shift your thoughts and awareness on *exploring* the reality that you do want to create. Your awareness of the new belief and reality that you do want to create will allow you to start perceiving it and will offer a new perspective for you. In time, you will attract this new belief and start to experience this new desired reality. As you do, it's no longer a belief, it will become truth, just as the old deep-rooted belief once was.

Tools like personal development, spirituality, self-awareness, and Law of Attraction are available to you to support you and empower you. Essentially, to living a better life, to transform your life, to create your life the way you want it to be. Sometimes, a person can take these teachings and use them against themselves. When teachings like these bring us fear or self-judgment, consider shifting your awareness to how these teachings could support you and empower you, versus self-judgment.

YOUR MIND CREATES YOUR REALITY

Remember, you are Creator within your own creation. However, everyone else is also Creator within their own creation. The reality you create within your own mind as you navigate through an experience, like a spouse having a stroke or health issue, is the reality that you are responsible for creating. This includes: the thoughts you think about the situation, the story you tell about it, whether you empower yourself or disempower yourself, and how you feel. It's understandable to feel moments of sadness, fear, or disappointment. Observe and acknowledge how you feel with compassion for yourself. Allow yourself the time you might need to adjust to the new situation, but then focus on applying these principles to create a reality of peace, empowerment, love, and well-being as you navigate through the situation.

We don't always know why things like this occur. Recently, I saw a friend while out running errands, whom I hadn't seen for several months since he had a stroke. I knew he had been paralyzed on one side of his body, and as we talked, it was evident that he was still experiencing some paralysis. As I talked with him, he shared with me how the stroke had changed his life, how he saw things differently, how he slowed down, how he found more meaning in things and how it, surprisingly to him, had transformed his life for the better.

He went on to say that the experience had been an *awakening* for him. I'm sure he wouldn't wish it on anyone or want anyone else to experience something as challenging and potentially life-changing as having a stroke. However, my friend has his own journey. We may never know why he had a stroke or how that was part of his soul's path to awakening. However, you can allow your loved ones to go through what they go through and know that you didn't cause it.

When something occurs and presents to you in your reality, you get to *choose* your perspective about it. And because you get to choose your perspective about it, you get to choose your experience. You get to create your reality. This is how you create your reality.

When something occurs, whether it is a disease—experienced by you or a loved one—or the death of a loved one, the loss of a job, end of a relationship, perceived failure, or any kind of challenging situation, these teachings are *not* meant to be used to then judge, persecute, shame, or disempower yourself. When you are choosing to be in relationships with other people, you are choosing to play with others who are also creating their reality. You are choosing to be a part of their journey too. Ultimately, these things are all happening for us and leading each of us to an awakening of who we really are and the power we have within to create our realities.

One might say, "I want my loved ones to awaken. I want them to know the power they have within them. I want them to know the truth of who they are, but I don't want anything *bad* to happen." These things are not bad or good. You have the ability to choose your perspective and *know* that everything is always happening *for* you, not *to* you. Allow your loved ones their journey too.

You have chosen to be in relationships with others, whether that is your family, spouse, significant other, friends, neighbors, co-workers, or those in your community. Because you chose to also be part of others' lives and journeys, there are things that are part of *their experiences* that are not for you to control; you must accept, observe, and remember that everyone's on their own path. However, regardless of what they choose, you always get to choose *your* perspective. Therefore, you always get to choose your experience. Therefore, you always get to choose the reality that you experience.

WHEN OTHERS DON'T UNDERSTAND YOUR AWAKENING

A student once asked me, "How would we transform the pain of nonacceptance from those we love?"

It is common on a path to awakening, transformation, or self-realization to feel that others in your life do not understand, accept, or approve of you. Many people in my own life did not understand when I left my corporate career to pursue my calling and live my life's purpose. When I started channeling The Council, I feared that not only would people not understand if I shared my channeling publicly, but that some of my friends and family might completely reject me. My greatest fear of all was that I would lose my relationship with my family, especially my dad, if they knew I was a channel.

My family was Christian and held a strong belief that Jesus was the only way and the only truth. Many people in my family had no awareness of things like channeling, meditation, reincarnation, or spirituality. Yet, they would jump to the conclusion that these things are opposed to their Christian beliefs. I struggled for a few years as to whether I would openly share The Council for fear of losing my family's love and acceptance of me.

One day, I had an experience where I saw myself at the end of my life having never brought The Council's wisdom to the world. I imagined what it would be like 30, 40, or 50 years from now to be at the end of my life wondering what my life could have been like and how many people would have missed out on The Council's wisdom had I not shared openly with others. It was clear; that just wasn't an option for me.

There was no way I could get to the end of my life not having shared The Council's wisdom with the world and everyone who was ready to receive it. In that moment, I knew that I had to *accept myself.* I had to be the one to approve of myself. I needed to understand *who*

I was and what I was here to do. And, even if no one else understood, even if my family couldn't accept it and didn't want to be in my life, I knew that *not* sharing The Council's wisdom and my channeling with the world was just not an option.

A week or so later, I released some channeling of The Council publicly on social media. The phone rang and it was my dad calling. He had *happened* to listen to my channeling, and he said, "I just don't get it. Why can't you use your own voice? Why do you have to call it The Council? I don't get it."

I took a breath and didn't react or go into fear that he wasn't going to accept me or approve of me. I remember that it was about me approving of me and accepting who I am. I said, "Dad, it's okay if you don't understand. You didn't understand when I did Information Technology Infrastructure consulting either." We both sort of chuckled as it was so true.

In that moment, there was total acceptance. There was total love. Even if he didn't understand, *I did*!

I had another experience with a close family member after openly sharing The Council. Surprisingly, I thought that family member would understand and have no concern with me channeling The Council. This person had always supported me, no matter what. I was very shocked to receive a text message one day that said, "I just can't have you in my life if you're going to be channeling. I don't agree with it."

I was shocked and completely surprised this person would react that way. I felt hurt and then very sad. I took some deep breaths to calm myself. I heard clearly a voice say to me in my head, "This is not about you. Stay in love and be love." After several minutes, I responded to his text message and said, "Okay, I love you."

In the couple of years that followed, I heard nothing from that person. I would text on holidays and birthdays and get no response or on occasion a simple *thanks*. I would feel sad sometimes about it, but kept doing my work with The Council, held the perspective that it wasn't about me, and continued to show up and be *love*.

One day, out of the blue, I received a message from that person. He said, "I was wrong. I am sorry. I couldn't be prouder of you and all you are doing to help people with your channeling." From that moment, it's been like nothing happened and our relationship has been filled with love, connection, and joy.

You might experience things like this where people don't understand, don't accept you or what you are doing, or don't approve of you. It's not about you. It's about what they're experiencing and where they are on their journey with their beliefs. Love them, but most importantly, *love yourself!* Don't let their beliefs or opinions be a reason for you to deny love for yourself.

Our next success principle will help you to come into the moment and find your power in situations like this.

All of your power is in the now moment.

*"All of your power is in the now moment. In the moment, you are
free. In the moment, you are whole. In the moment, there is only
love. In the moment, there is so much here for you. In the moment
is where you realize that you are everything you wish to be, you
already are. And in the moment is where you realize that it's all
within you, and it always has been. And let it expand and expand
and expand from there as every moment becomes even more
satiating, even more beautiful, even more magical as you
step into your mastery even more."*

— THE COUNCIL

When you're in the past, you are not in your power. When you
are trying to figure out the future, you are not in your power. All of
your power is in the now moment. If you're feeling guilty, resentful,
regretful, like you were victimized, or like you have failed, you are
denying your power in this moment. When you are in the past, in
an old story, feeling bad about something that happened, you're not
in your power.

The same is also true when you're trying to determine what you're
going to do in the future, worrying about what you're going to say,
how something is going to play out or what's going to happen in the
future; you are not in the now moment. You are not in your power.

When you are unconsciously trying to figure things out, worried
about the worst possible thing that might happen, you're not in your
power, and you can feel that you are not, which is what creates the

feelings of fear, stress, overwhelm, impatience, anxiety. This is very different, however, than using your imagination to explore creation and the realms of potential and possibilities, which we will explore more fully later in this book.

These emotions of guilt, regret, failure, worry, fear, and anxiety deplete your energy. You can see in others the energy of someone who is currently focused in the past or in the future and not present *in the now moment*. The same is true when you do become present to the now moment and begin to feel your power; it changes your energy.

BE IN THE NOW MOMENT

I remember years ago being at a family gathering, and an elder family member saying, "I had a lot of problems in my life, most of which never happened." He went on to say, "I worried about a lot of things in my life that never happened, robbed me of a lot of happiness." When I find myself unconsciously worrying about something, I often reflect on how it is robbing me of my happiness in this moment and find it much easier to choose to let go of the fear and allow my happiness here and now.

If you are overwhelmed, if you are frustrated, if you are feeling impatient, if you are feeling discouraged, depressed, any of those things, it is certain that you are thinking about the past or worrying about the future, and you are not in the now moment.

When you are in the moment, you feel a sense of peace, joy, happiness, and harmony. You can align to and allow your abundance and your well-being. When you are in the now moment, you can feel the infinite love that you are all around you. You can also tune in to the intuition, inspiration, and infinite intelligence that is available to you and always supporting you.

As you go through your day, if you notice that you are starting to feel overwhelmed, stressed, impatient, frustrated, *stop*! Take some deep conscious breaths. Move your awareness into this moment. Continue to breathe consciously and intentionally until you feel your awareness fully in the now moment.

If you notice you are feeling any of these unwanted emotions, ask yourself, "Where am I? How am I not being in the now moment?" Notice if you catch yourself in an old story about something that someone did to you in the past. Notice if you are holding yourself in an old habitual way of thinking thoughts like, "I wish I had the time back that I wasted. I wish I had the money back that I spent on this or that. I wish they would have done this or done that. I wish I had the body I used to have."

You can tell whether you're in the moment or not by how your body feels—your posture and the way you're carrying yourself. If you're sitting up straight with your shoulders back and your head held high, with a little twinkle in your eyes and a smile on your face, you're probably in the now moment and feeling your power in the now moment, which is visible in your body.

We can use the physical body to help us become present. Take a moment now. Sit up straight, engage your abdominal muscles, gently roll your shoulders back, gently elevate your neck and lift your head up high, feel a twinkle in your eyes as you gaze upward toward the sun, and bring a big smile to your face. Feel your power in your body. Feel your power in the moment.

Do this throughout your day. It gets easier and easier; you'll see. Most importantly, you will notice more quickly when you are not in your power and you can consciously, intentionally, come back into the now moment.

This can equip you to alleviate all suffering, struggle, overwhelm, worry, and fear in your life forever. You will never suffer again, you will never worry again, if you know that all your power is in the now moment. You would never worry about anything again if you lived this one success principle. If you know that you can always come into the now moment, take some deep conscious breaths, go from your head into your heart, feel your body, sit up straight, put your shoulders back, lift your head up high, put a smile on your face, come into the now moment, to fully summon all the energy that is here; everything is in the now moment.

We have the power in the now moment to transcend suffering and choose freedom. And yet, as much as you want freedom, oftentimes it is the very thing you deny yourself because you give your power away to circumstances outside of you, to the illusion of the reality that you are perceiving through your limited senses. You are powerful, and only you can set yourself free from all limitation, from all challenges and struggles, from any degree of suffering that you may be experiencing.

How do you set yourself free? Quite simply, stop giving your power away to things outside of you, to things in your news, to stories that you hold in your mind from people that you believe are powerful over you, to conditions that you think you cannot change or transform, because you are here as a Creator, a powerful Creator of your reality, and you couldn't be more free to create anything you wish to experience or desire to experience.

You are powerful. This is an opportunity for you, dear master, to set yourself free. Where do you hold yourself in bondage most of the time? In your mind, with the thoughts you think or the stories you tell yourself and what you believe about yourself.

You can set yourself free in any moment. Stop telling the story, stop holding on to the belief, stop repeating the limitation in your mind. If you think of a story of something that's happened that makes you feel powerless, stop telling the story. Simply stop. Catch yourself. Be conscious of when you're unconsciously holding yourself in a story that denies yourself freedom, that denies your power, that denies love.

It's a simple technique, but it may take many attempts to master. When you do, you'll realize that the stories you're telling are not real, are not true, were created by you in your mind to reaffirm to you your powerlessness, to reaffirm to you your belief that you are not free to create your reality exactly as you wish it to be.

Can you create your reality exactly as you wish it to be? Absolutely. Do you do so by forcing and efforting and stressing and worrying? No. You do so by co-creating with the consciousness and the energy that have created all the Universe here and now in this moment.

Years ago, when I read *The Power of Now* by Eckhart Tolle, I remember thinking to myself, *I don't get it*! I don't get how the "now" is going to make me more successful, create better relationships, or make me happier and healthier. I don't get it. But now, I get it! It's the greatest power we have. However, first comes the awareness, and oftentimes, our beliefs don't align or allow the new belief. Yet, once we begin to perceive the possibility, then we summon to us the experiences where a new, more powerful truth can become our reality. All the wisdom in the world doesn't change your life unless you apply it, and this one is *powerful*!

I often hear the question, "What about creating a catastrophic event and projecting it into the moment when it's not happening, creating a catastrophe that might happen in your future to avoid taking action in the present moment? How do you anchor yourself to the now moment when you observe yourself ruminating about what could happen? How do you let go of those old thoughts?"

Stop! Close your eyes, take three deep conscious breaths, move your awareness from your head and into your heart. Continue to breathe consciously and intentionally until you feel yourself come back into the moment and out of the story in your head.

It's simple. And yet, some people say, "I don't have time for three deep breaths. It's too easy. That's not going to work." However, in my own experience, as I have applied this teaching throughout my life, it's impossible for me to get to that third deep breath and not be in the moment.

Take the time to practice it now. Come into the moment. Take your first deep breath. Breathing in, one, two, three, hold it. Breathing out, three, two, one. Breathing in, one, two, three, hold it. Breathing out, three, two, one. Breathing in, one, two, three, hold it. Breathing out, three, two, one. You're in the now moment. I often find by the time I get to the third breath I want to take three more and then three more because it feels *so good*.

Sometimes I hear that same voice in my own head say, "This doesn't work. I don't have time for this. How are three breaths going to help?" After I take the second breath, my head might say, "Okay, fine, maybe I do feel a *little* better." And by the third deep breath, I am saying, "Oh here I am, that's it, I'm in the now moment." In my experience, this exercise is the best way that you can anchor in the now moment.

HOW TO EXPAND THE NOW MOMENT

Once, a student asked me the following question: "Considering that our power is in the now moment, I would like to understand why that is. What about daydreaming? What about affirmations? Can a person be in the now moment and visualizing at the same time?"

Visualizations, affirmations, and your imagination are all things that can help you to expand the now moment. However, you must be in the moment, not feeling bad about the past or worrying about the future, to expand the now moment. When you are in the now moment, you are not in resistance to the moment. You're not trying to make the moment different. You're not trying to make the past different. You're not worried and feeling powerless about the future. You're in the moment, you're in your power, and you get to think the thoughts that you choose, you get to choose the thoughts you think, you get to choose what you focus on. You get to choose what you're giving your attention to, the meaning you give it.

I love affirmations because you get to choose the thoughts, and often with affirmations, we are encouraged to affirm them out loud. "I am happy. I am healthy. I am loved. I am blessed. I am grateful. I am enough. I am worthy. I am important." Notice the difference in reading these affirmations and then reading them out loud. How do you feel in your body as you read them out loud? Does it feel empowering? Does it expand you? Does it expand the moment?

I believe when you speak affirmations out loud that it feels so good because every cell of your body *hears them.* I believe all the particles of infinite creation also hear them clearly. I believe all of the infinite intelligence all around you hears these affirmations and responds to make it your reality. One of my personal affirmations that I like to speak out loud and share with infinite intelligence is this: "Absolutely nothing could make me any happier than I am right now." I affirm it over and over until I feel the truth of it in every cell of my body.

You can do affirmations in your car. I love to do affirmations when walking my dog or out in nature. These powerful affirmations are an opportunity to expand your power in the now moment.

The 6th Dimension is the realm of imagination, pure potential, and infinite possibilities. The 3rd Dimension is based on separation, the 4th Dimension is based on transformation, the 5th Dimension is based on pure love, and the 6th Dimension is a formless dimension of imagination where we explore creation through potential and possibility to then move it into form as reality. We will cover this in greater detail later in the book.

When you are using your imagination to expand the now moment, you are accessing a higher level of consciousness where there is much more available to you and where things are more fluid and effortless. In these higher levels of consciousness, you are in the realm of pure potential and possibility. You are expanding the now moment. You are expanding your power and your consciousness in the now moment. Your imagination is available to you in this moment.

From the now moment, aligned to your power, you can also expand into your imagination to restore your innocence, wholeness, and divine perfection. An important part of self-realization is to integrate every part of you, including the precious, innocent little child within you. If you find yourself in a story about what your childhood was like, or your teenage years, other times of your life, don't judge yourself for being in the old story. Come fully into your power in the now moment and invite your younger self into this now moment with you.

As you expand the now moment, invite all of the experiences you've had throughout your life and every aspect of you to come into wholeness, Oneness, completeness, and into your power in the moment. There is a potential and a possibility in this now moment for you to bring every part of you into wholeness and completeness. You might choose to play in the 6th Dimension of imagination to access all of your potential and infinite possibilities in this moment, but that is where, *truly*, anything and everything becomes possible for you!

There is no need to make a big decision about anything; allow all things to be choiceless.

"You don't have to make any big decisions. You don't have to hold yourself in lack or limitation. You don't have to create separation. You are playing in the infinite possibilities that exist for you right here, right now, and in Divine right time, in the most easy, effortless, harmonious way the True Creation of that experience—that or something so much better—will present itself to you. It will just be choiceless. It will just be a yes!

"This is the same process with anything and everything because you are the powerful Creator of your reality. You are the powerful Creator of the masterpiece that is your life. It is time to fully express yourself, the inspiration that is you, the creativity that is you, the wisdom that is you, the knowledge that is you, the consciousness that is you."

— THE COUNCIL

What does *choiceless* mean? It means that you did not make a *big decision*. It means that the solution, answer, outcome, next step was obvious, logical, and unfolded perfectly, and you likely made the choice without even knowing it and were two, three, ten steps down your path before you even realized the decision had been made.

There is no need to make any big decisions. There's no need to make a big decision in any situation. Allow all things to be choiceless. The incredible Divine orchestration, grand manifestation, True Creation that so many have experienced by applying this success principle in their lives has been profoundly transformational. For me, this one principle has transformed my entire life beyond my wildest dreams, beyond what I ever could have imagined or thought to ask for.

If something in your life seems to be forcing you to make a big decision, in some way you are lowering your vibration and your consciousness. If it's a big decision, in some way you are imposing lack and limitation on your experience. You are holding yourself in a belief that there is a lack of time, options, opportunities, possibilities, or resources, so you must make a big decision, and make it now.

Fear equals fewer options. If you impose limitation on your situation and believe there is only one option, then you will instantly begin to feel fear. If you impose on your experience and believe that there is only one way or there's no way, it will also entangle you with fear, which will always move you into the lack, limitation, and separation experienced in the 3rd Dimension.

If you are making big decisions, in some way, you are limiting your power and you're limiting the power of the Universe. You are limiting the magic, the miracles, and the manifestations, and the experiences of True Creation that will often come completely *out of the blue* if you will allow things to be choiceless.

Choiceless has become a common reference with my students. They commonly will say, "it's just not choiceless" or "it was just choiceless." It's just not choiceless. When something is choiceless, you will often have already chosen and now you're moving ahead before you realize that you made a big decision. It will just be *choiceless*.

The Council asked us not to make any big decisions. Don't make any big decisions about your job. Don't make any big decisions about your relationship. Don't make any big decisions about where you live. Don't make any big decisions about anything. Allow things to be *choiceless*.

This is a common situation when someone is considering whether they should stay at their job or resign. The Council will say, "Don't make any big decisions. Allow it to be choiceless." One of my students was having a difficult time deciding whether she should leave her job. She said to The Council, "I am not sure if I should stay at my job or leave. I really want to quit my job. I had written my letter of resignation, but it feels like a really big decision because I don't know where the money is going to come from to get by without income. I want to start the new business, but I don't have time because of my work. However, I need income to get by for a few months while I start my new business." The Council said, "This is a big decision, which means that it's either not the right time, the right way, other options or information are coming, or events are being orchestrated *for you* that will allow this to be choiceless—when it's choiceless."

Not long after, the student excitedly came back to me and said, "I must share something so amazing with you. I didn't make any big decision, like The Council said. Yesterday, my boss came in *out of the blue* and said, 'We're eliminating your department, but we are giving you six months of severance pay.'" This was not an option she ever considered when trying to make a big decision.

If she had made a big decision out of fear and lack of options, she never would have received the severance to get her through for six months while she started her new business. If she had forced herself to make a big uncomfortable decision out of fear and lack of opportunities, she would have never allowed *exactly* what she wanted in a way she hadn't imagined possible, which was the opportunity to move out of her day-to-day job to have the opportunity, freedom, time, money, and resources to start her new business.

Another student was contemplating whether to leave her marriage or not. It was a *really* big decision. The Council responded saying, "Stay in your heart and know there is only love. Don't make any big decisions." She didn't see how it was possible to stay in the marriage any longer as she wasn't happy, but she was terrified to ask for a divorce.

Sometime later, the student reached out and said, "I must tell you that the *choiceless thing* really works! About a month ago, my husband walked in and out of nowhere said, 'I love you very much, but I don't want to be married anymore.' And I said, 'I love you, too, but I don't either.' So, we sat down, talked things out, it was a mutual, conscious uncoupling, and we have navigated through our separation with kindness, compassion, and ease. If I had tried to push it and force it and gotten all stirred up about it, I never would have been prepared for that moment."

NEW AWARENESS LEADS TO A NEW PERSPECTIVE

In early 2020, The Council specifically delivered a channeled message urging me and the community not to make any big decisions and specifically not until September 2020. This is a perfect example of how first you become aware of something new that allows you to have a new perspective, and then you draw new things to you that might never have been possible before, but they are *now* because you have a new awareness.

At the time, I was living in a home I loved and rented from a wonderful woman. She encouraged me to stay and rent the house as long as I wished, as the rental income was her retirement income. My lease was up at the end of September, but it wasn't a big decision as I didn't think I had any big decisions to make—I was staying in the house. In March 2020, The Council specifically said, "Don't make any big decisions till September." I thought to myself, "No problem, I don't have any big decisions to make."

Until one day in mid-August of 2020, I had a dream that I was moving. In my dream, I saw myself moving into a place with big windows, a white house, with wood trim. I would grab a box of the stuff I had moved to this new house; I would sweep it over a shelf and all my belongs would fall into perfect place in or on a shelf—exactly where it was supposed to be! I woke up from my dream, and my first thought was *I am so glad I'm not moving.* Two hours later, I got a message from the nice lady who owned the house that she was going to sell the house and was ending my lease the end of September. Suddenly, it felt like I had a lot of big decisions to make.

This was during the time of the Covid-19 pandemic, and in my area, it appeared as if there were absolutely no rentals available. I didn't want to buy a house at that particular time or in that particular area. But there were no rentals available. With each day that passed,

I felt like I was going to have to make a really big decision and soon. I kept focusing myself back into the wisdom of this success principle and told myself *let it be choiceless, let it be choiceless, let it be choiceless.* It's going to be choiceless. No big decisions.

It was now mid-September, and I was to move in a few weeks, but my landlord kindly offered me a little extra time, if I needed it. One evening, I was having dinner with some friends, and a friend of mine said, "Why aren't you moving to the *Valley*?" which is an area about 30 miles from where I was living. The first thought in my head was, "I can't move to the valley. I don't know anyone there. I don't want to move that far."

As I was reciting all the reasons in my head why I couldn't move to the valley, suddenly, it felt like I dropped into my heart and a powerful energy of joy came over me and I heard myself say, "I *could* move to the valley. I *could* move there. It would change my entire life if I could find a ranch there, and have a horse again, yes, I could live in the Valley."

Immediately after dinner, I rushed home and jumped online to look at houses in the valley. My soon-to-be house was listed *that* day. I went and looked, and two days later I signed the contract to move in. I moved into my beautiful ranch 18 days later and my new horse arrived two days after that. It was absolutely choiceless every step of the way. It changed my life forever. I am happier than I have ever been or could have imagined being. Out of the blue, the perfect solution presented itself, and everything was choiceless, from finding my house, to the moving company, to buying my horse, and beginning my new life. Of course, now I can't imagine living in my old house again.

Was I a little uncomfortable at times? Absolutely. But I remembered The Council's teachings. Don't make any big decisions. Don't believe in the lack and the limitation that everyone is telling me is happening, like there are no rentals, or housing prices are five times what they normally are because people are moving to the area because of the Covid-19 virus. I'm running out of time. I've got to find a place by this date, or I will have no place to live. This I know for sure—*there is* some greater intelligence that, if we are willing to allow it and allow it to be choiceless, can orchestrate things beyond our wildest dreams.

Allow it to be choiceless has become part of my language. I find myself saying often, *"It's just not choiceless."* In some cases, five minutes later, it might be choiceless. Five days later, it might be choiceless. It might be months later, but either way, allow it to be choiceless. And I promise you at some point it *will* be choiceless.

Sometimes things are being orchestrated *for us* in these situations and we can't see it yet. In my case, the house hadn't been listed yet, but the moment it was, this decision became choiceless. It was a big decision until the house came on the market and available and then, it was choiceless. That job position for you might not have been created *yet*, but when it is, it will be choiceless. The woman whose company hadn't yet decided to eliminate her department and give its employees severance found that when they did, it was choiceless for her.

CHOICELESSNESS IN RELATIONSHIPS

Sometimes in relationships, whether it's friendships, romantic relationships, or business relationships, things are being orchestrated in that other person's experience that allows a potential that never could have existed, like the woman whose husband came to her and said he wanted a divorce. One of my students asked, "I feel like The Council's wisdom has said to not make any big decisions, not to leave my relationship now, and to be the awakened one in a non-awakened family." This person was sharing that she had experienced some betrayal. It felt like a big decision to leave her marriage and husband and family, but it also seems like a really big decision to stay when she doesn't feel like she is where she belongs.

I have a good friend in my life who was in a long-term marriage and was very unhappy. His wife was an alcoholic and emotionally abusive. He was conflicted. He was loyal to his grown children and wanted to follow through on the agreement he made when he got married. For over a year, he kept saying, "Don't make any big decisions. Allow it to be choiceless."

One morning he awoke, and he heard clearly, "Today is *the day*." He said, "I grabbed my wallet. I walked out the front door with nothing but the clothes on my back and my wallet. I walked down the street away from my home—block after block after block after block until I saw a taxi. I got in the taxi, went to the airport, got on an airplane, and have never looked back."

I am not advocating for walking out on your marriage or leaving a relationship in this way. However, when sharing about *that day*, he said, "There was no thought about it. This energy moved me to walk out the door and leave *that day*, and in that moment, *it was choiceless*."

Allow it to be choiceless. There will come a moment—and you might not believe it's possible until you experience it, but it's true— there will come a moment where it will be absolutely choiceless. You will not even realize that you said it until it was said, did it until it was done, or chose it because it was just choiceless.

YOU HAVE A CHOICE

A student asked one time, "Doesn't that mean I have no choice?" To me, it means exactly the opposite: You are so clearly guided, supported, there's so much clarity, all the energy is in it, all the light is present in the moment that there is no choice to make, but you always have a choice. It is an absolute undeniable clarity, the energy and the light are clearly guiding you, and yes, there are lots of other potentials and possibilities, but in that moment, it is the highest divine expression for you. Doesn't that feel so empowering, uplifting, and inspiring?

Sometimes there appear to be deadlines when decisions have to be made by a certain time, like what appeared to be the case with the lease of my house. One student asked, "Would you say just wait out the time period until the moment the decision is required, where it becomes choiceless to make the decision less reactive?"

In the case of my house, my landlord told me in mid-August that I had a certain amount of time until I needed to move out. Later, I went back to her and asked if she would be willing to extend the lease a little longer if I needed it. And she did. At that time, I still didn't think there was any way I was going to be able to meet the extended deadline. I didn't think there was any chance I could find a house and move by that time. I was a bit worried about the deadline and if something would show up, or if I was just waiting around and no options would come in time.

Yet, everything I needed was there when I needed it, and the timing worked out perfectly. In fact, it was the time of the Covid-19 pandemic and lots of people were moving so it was months in some cases to get a moving truck. I only had *one day* in October that I *could* move because I had courses, classes, and events on all the other days. I called a couple moving companies and no one had any availability until November. A friend recommended a moving company I hadn't heard of in a city nearby.

I called and the nice lady at the moving company said, "I am so sorry, we've been booked for months." Then she said, "Hold on a minute." So I waited. She put me on hold for several minutes, and then came back on the phone and said, "We just had a cancellation, but this is *the only day* we have. You'll have to take it now." I knew, *I knew* what she was going to say. "It would have to be October tenth," she said. Everything is always working out for us.

When you live at this level of consciousness and awareness and allow things to be choiceless, everything always works out. *It does.* Now, here's the flipside of that. An example occurred when one of my students needed to be out of her house on a certain day, and that day was a few days away. She did not know where she was going. The place that she wanted to move into wasn't ready, and it wasn't choiceless. With just three days until she needed to move, she found an even better place than the one she was looking at, a much better place than where she was, and within three days she was able to get everything moved into a new place. However, it had just come available, in perfect, Divine right time. The Universe is efficient and expeditious. While our human minds might believe that it's *nice* to have several weeks or months' notice, *the Universe is efficient and expeditious!*

Sometimes there are more opportunities or more information coming available and it's happening behind the scenes. Your mind and senses might determine, from its perspective, that nothing is happening. However, if you will stay present, conscious, in your power, in the moment, you will always have everything you need, and everything will work out for you.

Other times, it's about asking for what you need. I'm a big believer in two things: the quality of your life is equal to the quality of your communication. I heard motivational speaker Tony Robbins make this statement years ago. In my experience, it's so true; *especially* when allowing things to be choiceness. I would add a second thing: The quality of your life is equal to your level of consciousness. It is especially important to stay in a higher level of consciousness when everyone else around you is in lack and limitation or worried about a particular deadline.

When you can stay in a higher level of consciousness, you can communicate clearly and powerfully. You can draw to you potentials and possibilities that might not be there for anyone else because of your higher level of consciousness, because of your ability to communicate consciously. Allow it to be choiceless. Trust yourself. Play with this! And just see how powerful it is in your life.

True Creation has no agenda.

"Feel an innocent excitement about whatever it is that you love or would love to experience without any attachment or expectation of a particular outcome. Know that when you are in a state of feeling pure love, what you want and need will come to you. The obvious, logical, next perfect step will present itself to you. You will take a step forward and the next step will place itself right beneath your feet as you follow your joy, as you follow your passion, as you experience pure love."

— THE COUNCIL

True Creation has no agenda. It is the expression of pure love within you and all around you. That pure love then moves into form as the highest expression of your soul's desires manifested and expressed in the most easy, effortless ways to surprise you, delight you, for you to play, for you to create more of *all that you are.* As you elevate your consciousness and your own vibrational frequency, you step into higher dimensions of existence where things that were once impossible for you now become easy, effortless, and harmonious.

It's time to let go of any beliefs of lack, limitation, and separation. It's time to let go of fear and worry. These things limit your human experience and cause frustration, resistance, stress, overwhelm, and cause you to doubt yourself as Creator within your own creation. Your elevated perspective of *what is* possible for you is the first step to uplifting and enriching your entire human experience into a new, more beautiful, more abundant reality.

True Creation has no agenda. There's no lack, there's no limitation, there's no delay, there's no force, there's no effort, there's no manipulation. It's *you* as the *pure love* that you are. Allow yourself to play and create in new levels of consciousness, without separation, without fear, without lack, without limitation.

It's as easy as not doubting and denying *who you are* and what is possible *for you*. It's as easy as coming into *this moment* and fully expanding, expressing, and experiencing yourself as Creator within your own creation. Everything is here, and now, and an extension of *you*. You are the consciousness and energy that is *in* everything and that has *created* everything. Come into Oneness Consciousness as the pure Source Energy that you are, where you do not need or want for anything because you *have it all*, you *are it all*.

When you do, you will experience more and more of the Divine plan expressing *through* you, and your soul's desires will unfold *for* you. No force. No effort. No manipulation. No need to control. No lack of anything ever. No experience of limitation. No fear. No worry. No stress. No resistance. No judgment of yourself or any other.

Your highest potential is to experience your soul's desires in physical form, to live your life's purpose, to remember the plan for your life. There is a Divine plan for *your life*, and *you have chosen it*. You are the Divine expressing yourself in the world. You don't *want* for anything, you *are* everything. Allow your soul's desires to take the highest form because *that form* is beyond what you could ever think to ask for with your limited human senses.

A HIGHER VIEWPOINT

There is a grander perspective. Your higher self is that grander perspective, is that higher viewpoint, is in a continual state of Oneness with Source, God, the Divine, the grander part of you. When you're allowing the force field of consciousness that is you, you are connected to everything and everyone. Allow True Creation to reveal itself to you. Play, create, and *choose* the experiences that you want to have for you. Follow the energy and let the light guide the way.

True Creation is pure love. There's so much power in knowing that. There is so much power in knowing that pure love is in everything. True Creation unfolds with effortless ease when you come into pure love and allow pure love to express through you in the highest form, without lack and limitation. Choose to *be* pure love, to *feel* pure love, to *express* pure love, knowing that True Creation has no agenda.

RELEASE AGENDAS AND EXPECTATIONS

There is an infinite intelligence that has a much grander perspective of who we are, where we are, and what is possible. We are often looking at *what is* through limited human senses of what we see, hear, taste, touch, and smell. We often think we know what would make us happy, but it is limited to what we think is possible in our given situation or circumstances. Your soul or higher self is that higher perspective and knows who you are, what's possible for you, and knows the most easy, effortless, harmonious, and joyful way to move you into that experience.

True Creation has no agenda because it knows that the consciousness and energy that creates everything is within everything and always available in every moment. When understanding that True Creation has no agenda, consider replacing the word *agenda* with the word *resistance*, or limitation, or attachment. True Creation has no resistance, no limitation, no expectation, no attachment. You do not have to experience lack, limitation, separation, or frustration to allow the expansion of all that you have become and attracted to you through the process of True Creation. When you allow True Creation, what you want and need show up even before you know you need it. When you allow True Creation, it comes to you and—it's a yes!

If you have an agenda and expectation, it is often because you are lacking what you think you need. Because of the limitation or fear you are experiencing, you want your creation now, which will immediately entangle you in separation, lower your vibration, and limit the energy you are summoning in that moment. You can literally feel resistance and then your logical mind takes over and tries to force an outcome. In this example, your mind can only perceive that there is only one way for your manifestation to come, or in some cases, no way for it to happen, so you begin to push, force, effort, struggle, and suffer.

Your own resistance creates fear, and fear equals fewer options. If there's only one way, you're going to be holding yourself in a lower level of consciousness of limitation and separation where you can't experience the True Creation that will surprise you, delight you, and deliver to you *the* most amazing things. True Creation often comes *out of the blue.* Not because you're not prepared, not because you're not in alignment with it, not because you haven't felt your way into the experience of it, not because you don't have clarity about what you love, but out of the blue, because there is no struggle, no lack of, no resistance, no limitation, no expectation, no attachment, no agenda of how, when, and where it must happen.

Your soul has the grandest view, knows how to inspire desire within you for the very purpose of your expansion. True Creation comes forth from your soul for the purpose of your expansion. True desire comes forth from your soul because your soul desires the data and information that comes with creating that desire in your reality. If your soul can inspire a desire within you, your soul knows exactly how to deliver that to you, and your soul knows exactly the perfect manifestation to expand every area of your life.

Let go of the resistance. Let go of the expectation. When your soul inspires a desire within you, go into your imagination, play, and explore all sorts of potentials and possibilities. Allow yourself to play from a state of innocence and with a sense of wonder and curiosity without imposing resistance, expectation, or an agenda of when and how it needs to happen.

Instead of saying *I want to manifest this or manifest that,* or *I need this or I need that,* consider making it a statement. Say, *how fun would it be to experience this or that.* If you need a vacation because you are so tired, burned out, exhausted, instead of saying I need a vacation, shift your awareness. Consider how fun would it be to go on vacation. Can you feel the vibrational difference between these two statements?

When you are frustrated and exhausted and say, I need a vacation, it's coming from lack, limitation, and resistance. When you consider the question, how fun would it be to go on a vacation, you feel a sense of curiosity, playfulness, excitement, passion, and expansion.

Get yourself into alignment with the essence of True Creation, which is the essence of curiosity, excitement, and fun, and comes from a place of wonder, expansion, and exploration. Take any desire you have and form it into this question: "How fun would it be to experience . . . ?"

Here is the important part: After you allow yourself to play in the potentials and possibilities, don't introduce resistance into your experience by talking about why you can't have the experience you desire. As you go throughout your day, continue to pursue what you're passionate about, pursue what you're excited about, move in the direction of the experience you desire, do what you love, do what brings you joy—without an agenda, resistance, and the expectation of exactly how and when it happens—or the expectation that it's not possible for you.

ALLOW THE PROCESS

Sometime around 2013, I woke up in the middle of the night and I heard the words, "Sara Landon is a spiritual teacher." I heard the words in my head, but they came to me, not from me. At the time, I was working in the corporate world, and the desire to become a spiritual teacher made no sense to me and seemed completely impossible.

While the idea was exciting to me, the only person I knew of who was a spiritual teacher at the time was Wayne Dyer. My mind instantly stepped in and offered me a number of reasons why being a spiritual teacher like Wayne Dyer was impossible. Wayne Dyer had been doing it for decades, he was a doctor and had his PhD, so people listened to him. He had experience, accreditations, a publisher, was on public television, and had an audience.

Who was I to think I could ever be a spiritual teacher like Wayne Dyer? I saw no path for the desire to become a reality. However, the desire came from pure, innocent inspiration. While my mind continually offered thoughts of doubt, I could not stop thinking about those words, "Sara Landon is a spiritual teacher." I would have been unable to figure out how it was possible. However, within a few years of my soul inspiring this desire within me, I had left my corporate career, was channeling The Council, and teaching courses and workshops on spirituality. Within 10 years, I had a global community of students, published three books with Wayne Dyer's publisher, and was considered by many to be a spiritual teacher.

I wasn't consciously aware at the time, but without knowing what I was doing, I began allowing the magnificent process of True Creation to unfold. I imagined how fun it would be to be a published author. How fun would it be to teach courses and classes? How fun would it be to connect with people all over the world and share The Council's teachings? How fun would it be to talk about spirituality and consciousness all day? How fun would it be to really explore what it means to live our highest potential and then get to cocreate and play and share with people all over the world how we do that?

It was pure, innocent inspiration. I had no agenda around it, only a passion that didn't waver. Yes, I really wanted to create the experience. Yes, I wanted to manifest it, but it came as an inspiration. It came as a vision. It came from my soul. My mind never would have conceived it was possible for me.

While the experience of True Creation and the realization of my dream has been so magical, the journey to that desire is *the very best part.* If someone had told me back in 2013 that I could snap my fingers and be a spiritual teacher, in that moment, I would have said, "Just make it my reality *now!*" However, I would have missed all the magic, miracles, adventures, love, beauty, fun, and joy along the way. For me, the best part of all has been the people I have met on my journey. In my own experience, the connection with others has been a very special part.

It is about who you become along the way. You are everything you wish to be, you already are. However, the unfolding and the discovering of who you really are and what is truly possible for you is the hidden treasure, the kingdom, the happily ever after that inspires so many of our books, fables, movies, and sagas.

Once you experience True Creation without lack, limitation, and resistance, it is life-changing, and you will see that True Creation has no agenda. Sometimes things work out exactly as we imagine them to be, and that's perfect. If it doesn't, there are gifts, there is beauty, there is love, there are adventures, there are experiences that you're going to receive along the way *in addition* to the experience of the True Creation of your soul's desire. Along the way, you become more of all that you are and collect even more data, information, and wisdom that will lead to even more expansion.

SURRENDERING IS OPENING AND ALLOWING

A student once asked me, "Is True Creation and not having an agenda the same as surrendering?" Years ago, I thought that I could *outsmart* the Universe. I would think to myself, I am going to *surrender,* and then what I want will come faster! I'm going to surrender, because if I surrender, then the Universe will give me what I want!

Other times, when I contemplate the act of surrendering, I arrive at a place of feeling like nothing I do is working, so I am going to just give up. I just let go of what I want and just give up because it's too painful to keep wanting it and not having it. And for most of us, that doesn't feel very good. There's a reason. There's a reason you have the dream in your heart. You wouldn't have the dream in your heart if it wasn't possible for you. However, you weren't meant to push, force, struggle, effort, and suffer your way to your creations.

I don't think of surrender as *giving up.* For me surrender comes when you have done all that you can do from your human's perspective, and you open and allow a higher power or perspective. There is a power that is you, that is more than just this human that you know as you having this human experience. There's a reason that your dream is in your heart.

There's a *reason* this dream is in *your* heart. When you open and allow a higher power, higher perspective, infinite intelligence, the Universe, you allow True Creation, which has no limitations. True Creation might deliver it exactly how you see it. It might be so much better than how you imagined it. Let go of the resistance and *surrender the struggle.* Surrender the resistance. Surrender the need to push, force, and effort. Surrender the frustration with how long you have been trying to make this happen. When you surrender, there's peace, there's joy, there's ease, there's harmony, there's excitement again, there's innocence again. Now you can allow True Creation without an agenda.

You are surrendering the struggle. You are letting go of the resistance. Surrender the struggle. Be in your joy, be in peace, be in this moment, and you will open up to being able to clearly receive the next perfect step. And things begin to show up for you.

That leads to the question: Can surrender also be giving your power away to something outside of you? True Creation is not about saying, "I'm not powerful enough, so I'm going to surrender to something *outside* of me that's more powerful than me."

True Creation is divine co-creation with every part of you. There is the part of you that is the incredible, extraordinary human in physical form on Earth at this time. And there's the part of you that is Pure Source Energy that stayed in nonphysical and has a grander perspective where everything is known. True Creation is about bringing together every part of you.

When you experience True Creation, you're not *giving* your power away to something outside of you that's bigger than you. You're integrating the magnificent human that you are with the powerful Source Energy that you are. In your connection to Source Energy, you lack for nothing, you need for nothing, there is no struggle. You're in your power. It's all here for you. Then your only job is to receive and allow the surprise, delight, excitement, wonder, magic, miracles, and True Creation to present itself to you.

Stillness is the access point to acceleration.

"Stillness is not only the access point to acceleration. Stillness is the access point to your power. Stillness is the access point to light, to enlightenment, to realization, and then the moment expands as magic and miracles and manifestations and True Creation presents itself to you in this expanded moment that you have created."

— THE COUNCIL

How often do you find yourself running around chasing after everything you think you want and need, trying to push and force, struggling and efforting to make something happen? If you will just stop, sit quietly, close your eyes, take some deep breaths, feel the sunshine on your face, and find a moment of stillness, all the resources, opportunities, ideas, inspiration, and manifestations that you have been chasing will come to you. Stillness is the access point to drawing your destiny to you.

If you will teach yourself to stop, find the inner state of stillness, and take some deep breaths, reality begins to move through you, your destiny comes to you, magic and miracles present themself to you, and the grand manifestations that have been here all along begin to move into your experience. There is power in stillness and presence. There's clarity. There's ease.

You are worthy of stillness. You are worthy of slowing down. You are worthy of putting some space around yourself to slow down and take some deep breaths, find some moments of stillness, and allow yourself to receive everything that is here for you. You are worthy of having it all and it's all here for you. Stillness is the access point to acceleration because in stillness you can breathe yourself into your power. Take three deep breaths, go from your head down into your heart. All of your power is in the now moment. Slow down. Come into your power. Slow down. Let it come to you.

Don't go out and try to make something happen from your place of limitation or resistance or discomfort or anger or frustration or shame. Breathe yourself into your power. Breathe yourself back into your power in this moment. All of your power is in the now moment, and all that matters is you being in your power in this now moment. Come back into your power first, then expand into an inner state of stillness, and the rest will become clear to you.

Stillness is a feeling of Oneness with All That Is. It is a feeling of expansion. The expansion you are feeling is the expansion of your force field of consciousness and the energy you are summoning is that experience of stillness. When you first become aware of stillness, it might be easiest to do when sitting quietly and closing your eyes. However, in time, you will find stillness while also in motion.

Take a moment. Focus yourself into the stillness in this moment while also feeling the expansion of all that you are. Stillness is the access point to acceleration. However, feel such presence and expansion in the stillness that you really aren't attached to the acceleration. Stillness is the access point to manifestation. But feel such presence and a fullness and Oneness in the stillness that you're not attached to the manifestation. Stillness is the access point to True Creation, but feel such presence, Oneness, expansion that you're not attached to the True Creation. Stillness is the access point to realization, but feel so expanded in this moment of stillness and so satiated, such freedom and Oneness, that you're not attached to the realization, *it just is.*

Realization just is because it is your natural state of being. You don't have to force your way to realization. It is a natural unfolding of your way of being if you will allow it through expansion and stillness.

Stillness is the access point to acceleration, manifestation, True Creation, and realization. And if you know that stillness is the access point to acceleration, then it doesn't matter when the acceleration occurs, it's all now. It doesn't matter when the manifestation occurs because it's all now. It doesn't matter when the True Creation presents itself because it's all now. It doesn't matter when you experience the realization because it's all now. When you are in a state of stillness, you're never separate from anything. You can create the illusion of its absence through your thoughts and focus, but you're never separate ever.

If you're willing to accept stillness for its power, it's going to lead you to the manifestation, the True Creation, the realization, the acceleration. Allow the unfolding, the journey, the time of gestation until it's the obvious, logical next perfect step. If what you want to create is *big*, perfect. Come into the power of stillness, enjoy the journey to becoming, enjoy the unfolding until what you desire is the obvious, logical next perfect step.

Stillness doesn't mean that you are sitting still. It means that you are consciously, intentionally focused into the vibrational frequency of Oneness. Nothing is outside of you. You're fully in the realization of the forcefield of consciousness that is you, and that part of you that is not separate from anything, ever.

STILLNESS IS THE ACCESS POINT TO ACCELERATION

I must admit, I'm a former Type A. I was the type who was going to *make it happen* and do it my way. I always had a plan and a backup plan and a backup plan for that. I was always busy, always getting stuff done. I found pride and some level of worthiness in being able to do it all by myself. Then, I started channeling The Council and they presented the awareness that "stillness is the access point to acceleration." I could literally hear that thought in my head while in channel say, "Stillness? That sounds so boring!" However, such is the process that first you have an awareness of something, then you start to perceive it or perceive things from a different perspective, then you start to experience it. Only then does it become your reality and the belief becomes truth.

Now, I am the *queen of stillness*. I love to focus into that powerful state of stillness when I am driving, writing, teaching, cooking, walking my dog, riding my horse, or playing. Stillness can be incredibly satiating as you feel yourself expanding into the moment, feeling into that stillness, feeling all your power, wholeness, completeness, perfection, radiance, brilliance.

Sometimes stillness is sitting and closing your eyes, taking some deep breaths, slowing everything down, putting space around you, and visualizing that you are expanding the force field of consciousness that you are until you feel that there is nowhere that you are not, that everything is within you and available to you. Sometimes stillness is a focused, intentional slowing down, expanding the moment, connecting to everything, coming into Oneness, and allowing yourself into a state of Oneness, connected to All That Is, in the absolute stillness, in your own perfection.

Other times, it's finding those moments where you're driving the car, doing the dishes, cooking dinner, doing work, writing, teaching, doing manual labor, whatever you might be doing. Stillness is always there! Stillness is the intentional connecting into your Oneness. I often prefer those moments when I can *really* sit and connect into everything and be so tuned in to All That Is. And there is mastery in finding that place of stillness, aligning to stillness, that state of being no matter what you're doing.

Once you embrace this success principle, you begin to quickly feel when you are not in a place of stillness, saying to yourself, "I am going to *make it happen*, force it to happen, figure it out, it's going to be my way or the highway." Instead, allow the inspired action and inspiration that comes from aligning to that place of stillness.

It's common to come to a place of stillness and the inspired action might come and you are staying in balance and harmony as the momentum kicks in, as the acceleration occurs. The Council has said in those moments of the manifestation, of the realization, of the acceleration, slow down, slow down, slow down, slow down, take it all in, really receive all of it.

One of my favorite things that The Council says is, "Be so satiated in the moment that you don't want the moment to end." You are full, filled up—to be satiated is to be full, to be filled up. When this moment is so full and you are so filled up with your being, in your experience of wholeness and Oneness and completeness and perfection, and it is so satiating that you don't want this moment to end, and that moment just expands and expands and expands, to me, *that's stillness.*

Stillness is the access point to acceleration, manifestation, True Creation, realization. Let your destiny come to you, let the dream come to you, let the grand manifestation come to you, let the True Creation present itself to you, let it all come *to you.* Imagine that you are sitting on a park bench in a peaceful, lovely location on a beautiful, warm, sunny day. You can feel the sunshine on your face, smell the freshly trimmed green grass. In front of you there is a pond or a lake with swans and ducks floating about. You can hear children playing and watch as dogs play together at the park. Happy people are walking through the park. It's perfect and you feel so satiated sitting there on the park bench.

As you sit there on the park bench, you are allowing. Instead of running around all over town chasing down what you think you want and need, your dreams come to you. True Creation comes to you. Your desires present themselves to you. Experiences come out of the blue to you. Think about it like this: When you are running around all over the place, your dreams must chase after you. The manifestation you desire is chasing after you as you run all over town.

You are taking *massive, determined action.* You're going to make it happen. You're going to make it happen your way, on your timeframe, and you are running all over town, making it happen, pushing, forcing, efforting, bulldozing, in resistance, frustrated. You are wondering to yourself, "Why isn't it happening? How do I make it happen?" Meanwhile, your dreams, your destiny, your future is chasing after you as you run all over town. Until you *stop* and you sit down on the park bench. You remember the power of stillness and fill yourself up with the moment, and in stillness, you find yourself totally satiated, and then here comes that experience of True Creation that says, "Oh, thank goodness you sat down! I've been chasing you around all day." That's one of my favorite examples because *I* can *definitely* relate to that one! How about you?

STILLNESS VS. THE NOW MOMENT

What is the difference between the now moment and stillness, stillness and the expansion of the now moment? Stillness is the expansion of the now moment. Stillness is the gateway, the portal, the doorway to expansion and Oneness. The instant manifestation of stillness is complete and total Oneness, and in that, you expand.

The now moment is about coming into your power, coming fully into your power. Stillness is about expanding into every part of you within all of creation, where you are the consciousness and the energy that creates everything, where it's all within you and available to you, and you aren't separate from anything, anywhere. It's all here and it's all here for you. It's about expanding your consciousness into Oneness. The experience of stillness is complete and total Oneness, the integration of every part of you with All That Is, which to me is the experience of self-realization.

One of my students explains it like this: "Let the presence make the plan." I encourage you to play with all of this and have fun exploring stillness. Play with it! Don't take this all so seriously. Don't judge yourself. Allow the awareness to move you into a new level of perceiving so you can experience self-realization and allow it to become your own truth.

Channeled Activation for Exploring Your Creation

We are so pleased and delighted to have the opportunity to speak with you all on this fine and glorious day indeed. We remind you that while our words to you are important, this is a vibrational experience of remembering the truth of who you really are, why you are here, and all that you intended when you chose this magnificent life experience.

You truly are a master here to experience life in all its glory, in all its perfection. Every potential and possibility are here for you to choose and to create your reality. You are exploring creation in physical form. You are exploring the power of consciousness and energy to create in physical form realities, masterpieces, manifestations. And sometimes those manifestations and experiences of True Creation, they're already here, they're already a part of you, but you can't even perceive them until you allow yourself into the awareness of how worthy you are, how loved you are, how deserving you are of every dream in your heart. The dream was inspired within you from your soul, and your soul always knows the highest expression of all that is possible for you. And indeed anything, everything is possible for you.

You cannot look at someone else's experience and go, "Why can't I have that? Why can't I do that?" It is about going within in those moments of stillness, connecting into the infinite intelligence that is all around you and always available to you, and feeling into the highest expression of the truth of who *you* are, the greatest potential for *your* highest expression.

Everything is potential and possibility. You are here to live fully and play in the potential and possibilities. You are here to love fully in the knowing of your worthiness and your perfection and your wholeness and completeness. You are here to be all that you are, the magnificent human that you are, the powerful Source Energy that you are, the eternal being that you are. You have drawn all this to you at this time to experience the integration of every part of you—*self-realized*.

When you ask, "What is self-realization?" the answer lies in the energy of the very words themselves. As you say them out loud and you feel for the truth within them, you are aligning every cell of your body into your wholeness, your completeness, your perfection, your magnificence, your radiance, to align with the master that you are. Self-realized. Self-realized. Self-realized. And so it is.

We are always with you. We are always available to you. We do not choose for you. We do not control you. Nothing outside of you is determining what you should do. You are the powerful Creator of your reality. You are a master. You have come forth to create your reality. You have come to live fully, to love fully, to be all that you are.

You choose from the infinite potentials and possibilities. You choose to come into those moments of stillness, to connect with All That Is, to allow the dream in your heart, the deepest desires of your soul for the very purpose of your expansion. You choose to allow the inspiration of your highest potential. You choose what would be fun for you. You choose what it is you want to experience. And all of us on this side, we are here loving you, responding to you, supporting you, guiding you, offering you a grander perspective so that you do not lose your way, so that you do not dim your light, so that you do not play small, so that you self-realize to be all that you are and create as the powerful Creator that you are.

You have chosen to be a master. Live this fully. It truly is fun!

We have enjoyed this so very much. You are everything you wish to be. You already are. It is all within you. It always will be. We love you, we love you, we love you, dear master. And with that, we are complete.

Review: Exploring Your Creation

SUCCESS PRINCIPLE #9: All of your power is in the now moment.

- You have no power when thinking about the past and feeling guilty, regretful, resentful, victimized, or like you failed.

- You have no power when you're anxious and worried about future events.

SUCCESS PRINCIPLE #10: There is no need to make a big decision about anything; allow all things to be choiceless.

- If you feel like you are making a big decision, in some way you are imposing lack and limitation on your experience. It could be lack of time, lack of options, lack of money. Feelings of lack lead to fear. Fear equals fewer options.

- When it's choiceless, you will likely have already decided/chosen and are moving ahead before you realize it was choiceless and not a big decision.

SUCCESS PRINCIPLE #11: True Creation has no agenda.

- Connect to your soul, which has the greatest viewpoint and can inspire desire within you for the purpose of your expansion.

- True Creation can feel like innocent excitement, wonder, curiosity. Ask yourself, "How fun would it be to experience . . . ?" Then, notice that there is no resistance, limitation, expectation, or attachment.

SUCCESS PRINCIPLE #12: Stillness is the access point to acceleration.

- Imagine sitting on a park bench feeling totally satiated, and your destiny comes to you on that park bench with effortless ease versus your destiny chasing after you as you run all over town trying to make something happen.

- Stillness is found through the expansion of the present moment and allows you to reach the access point for acceleration, manifestation, True Creation, realization, and transformation.

PART IV

EXPRESSING
YOUR TRUE SELF

"The whole Universe and all the energy within it is here for you and available for you to create your masterpiece, to create your reality, and all that is asked of you is to allow it, to summon it into your reality so you can experience True Creation as the master that you are. This entire planet is here for you. This entire Earth experience and everything that that includes is here for you.

"There is a continuation of everything, there is an expansion of everything, and you understand that there is a multidimensional nature to you. But this is the one and only life that you are focused on now, and this is the time to move fully into every potential, every possibility, open every timeline and begin to play in those infinite possibilities as you summon the energy to create your masterpiece, as you summon the energy to bring Heaven to Earth, as you summon the energy to create paradise on Earth, to explore every paradise on Earth that is here for you, and then to come together, these masterpieces that you are and the lives you have created, and to expand the potentials and the possibilities for all of humankind."

— THE COUNCIL

In this final section, let's explore the success principles for expressing your true self. This is about expressing yourself without limitation, fully expressing all that you are, the integration of every part of you, the pure love that you are, the self-realized master that you are, and the principles to help you do that in the most efficient, expeditious, advantageous ways. To express yourself means to not limit any part of you, to not hold back or play small, to not dim your light, but to allow yourself to be authentic, open, innocent, and unique.

As you begin to focus your attention on fully allowing yourself to express all that you are, I predict it will almost instantly begin to transform your life in the most amazing way so that you *can* live and create the life of your dreams. These success principles have been the key for me and so many others to really create our best life, a life that we love, and in some cases—I know it's true in mine—a life beyond what I ever could have thought to imagine.

Please take these principles, apply them in your life, watch the miracles and the magical things that unfold and present themselves to you. Have fun with all of this! I feel it's important to share with you stories of how the success principles are helping people do *just that*— create their best life. There is nothing better than knowing that these principles are working, in action, creating incredible manifestations for people, allowing them to start living their best lives right now.

During the live presentation of the course this book is based on, one student wrote to me and said, "Just prior to hearing you live on today's session, I was looking at trips to Maui, but I was panicking about the cost, while also knowing that our family really needed some time together. My husband is an actor and works in another city five days a week. The discussion during the live session really gave me perspective and shifted my thinking. I shifted into feeling that we really do have more than enough to go on the trip. I began to connect with the joy and excitement of the trip instead of all the things that will need to happen to get us there. As soon as the session was over, my husband called and said that he had received an email that he had a very large residual check being deposited from a McDonald's commercial that he filmed two years ago, and we did not have to worry about the money for the trip! Thank you for this amazing shift that led to a miracle in my life."

She continued saying, "When you begin to experience and live them, you see *instantaneously* examples of them working in the present moment." This beautiful share absolutely made my day when I received her email. I am thrilled to share it with you as an example of *what is* possible and happening for people who apply these success principles.

I also received a message from a woman in Australia. She not only shared an incredible experience, but also how the unfolding of her experience incorporated many of the success principles at play in her life. She said, "In alignment with the 15 Success Principles for Self-Realization, I am sharing an experience I had a couple of weeks ago and it wasn't until I wrote it out that I realized the level of integration that I had of The Council's wisdom. It was truly a culmination of 12 Success Principles out of 15 in one experience—whoa!

"As I describe my experience, it may seem as if it was robotic and there was separation, but there truly wasn't. It came with no resistance, no judgment, only acceptance of what is, and there was flow. It really was harmonious and effortless, which is the experience of Success Principle Number 8.

"A few weeks ago, a Category 3 cyclone was moving through my city. However, because of The Council's Success Principles, I was reminded that no matter what 'chaos' is happening around me, I can be at peace and harmony, with me, now. This helped me to see how to apply Success Principle Number 4, *What you focus on and the meaning you give it is creating your reality,* and Success Principle Number 9, *All of your power is in the now moment.*

"In the moment, I found stillness, Success Principle Number 12, as I took the time to pause and reflect on this. Suddenly, more principles came flooding in. I heard and knew that all energy moves through me, and I must first create it within me, Success Principle Number 6. I also knew in that moment that I am the Creator within my own creation of my reality, Success Principle Number 3.

"To fully allow my creation in form, I knew I had to choose my state of consciousness in order to fully summon the energy for my creation into form, Success Principle Number 14. I said to myself,

'I can have peace and harmony within me now. All is well, and is aligned with the energy,' Success Principle Number 7.

"As the cyclone approached, I was able to align to a higher level of consciousness, knowing my well-being was assured, Success Principle Number 15, despite that all the talk on the radio, the TV, and social media was fear based. It felt natural to choose to see this experience from a grander perspective and the magic presented itself up in the sky to me.

"Around 1 P.M. on the day the cyclone was to hit, I got the feeling to go to a nearby shop for a few last-minute purchases. The cyclone was due around 7 P.M. Although I wasn't desperate to have the items, I followed the energy and guidance anyway. I arrived at the store, and it was already closed. I remembered Success Principle Number 5 and knew that this was happening for me, not to me. On my way back to my house, the whole sky was dark gray and stormy. However, I looked up and above *my house* there was blue sky. The sun was even shining on *my house*. If I hadn't followed the energy and guidance to go to the *closed shop,* I may not have ever seen the magic in the sky. Within 5–10 minutes, the sky changed to stormy again, but the magic continued. Twice more throughout the afternoon, I looked outside to see blue sky and the sun shining over my house.

"More magic and miracles presented themselves to me as the adventure continued. Over 68,000 homes in my area lost power and some were out of power for six days. My house did not lose power at all; not even a flicker. My house was in a one-kilometer radius where the homes were not affected by the cyclone, and no one lost power. To add to the dramatic excitement, our city was experiencing a heatwave. Therefore, people outside the one-kilometer radius not only had no power, but no refrigeration to keep their food fresh and no air conditioning to keep themselves cool.

"The cyclone came and went and in *my creation of reality,* the outcome was: There was no damage to my house and property, we didn't lose power, my family was safe, my dogs were safe, moments of beautiful sunshine and blue sky appeared, and the intensity of the cyclone was less than reported by the authorities. This experience really showed me that living the wisdom, The Council's wisdom, really does create magic and miracles . . . every day!"

In addition to these incredible shares, others who participated in the live sessions asked questions that helped us to expand our awareness and more fully integrate the wisdom in the Success Principles. One participant asked the question, "If we were here to expand consciousness and consciousness is always expanding, does this have anything to do with us feeling like we're not enough? Because there never seems to be an end of *always more.* Is Source ever happy with enough? Or is it just a limited viewpoint that is difficult to understand with our human mind?"

We are in this experience for expansion. We are always creating. If we are *here* in this human experience, we are here for expansion, we are here to express all that we are, and we are here to choose the experiences that we want to have.

Each day in some way, you are creating. As you continue your journey through the human experience, you are more fully expressing all that you are, you are more fully aware of the experiences that are here for you to choose, and you are more fully expanding.

You *are* everything that you wish to be. You already are. *And* you are always expanding and becoming more.

As you navigate through your human experience, take the time to consciously be aware of what you are creating. Begin by moving into a higher level of consciousness. Feel yourself in the moment being totally satiated, which is to feel into the fullness of all that you are. Come into the knowing that you are more than enough, nothing needs to change. Focus yourself into a feeling that everything around you and within you is here supporting you, that everything is potential and possibility here for your choosing. Remember that life is meant to be a grand adventure.

YOU ARE WORTHY

Your human experience is not a quest or a test to do something that will finally make you worthy. That's not the purpose of expansion. It is the journey of becoming, although you are everything you wish to be. There is nothing that could ever happen in this human experience that could ever threaten your worthiness. There is nothing you can achieve or accomplish in this human experience that could ever make you more worthy than the divine, inherent, infinite worthiness that is the truth of you.

Think of your own experience before the 1990s and early 2000s, before we had cell phones, applications, social media, artificial intelligence, and technologies that allow us to connect real-time with video and audio to anyone in the world. We are expanding technologically. We are expanding in research, information, and innovation.

We are expanding in our ability to live at higher levels of competency and comfort. Think about how many people had running water, electricity, indoor plumbing, and refrigeration 100 years ago versus now. Think about how many homes had color televisions prior to 1970 and how many homes have televisions, streaming video, wi-fi, and Internet connections now. We as humanity are expanding.

Our potentials and possibilities are expanding, not because we weren't enough before we had televisions or cell phones, but because it expands our capabilities and opportunities. It expands the potentials and possibilities for how we express ourselves. The expansion of consciousness does not have to be a constant struggle or quest to be more because we are not enough or somehow unworthy as we are. It as an expansion of potentials and possibilities for what we can create in our experience.

The journey through the human experience is meant to be a grand adventure that contributes to our own unique expansion, expression, and experiences. It also contributes to the expansion, expression, and experiences of the collective. This leads us to our next Success Principle.

Life is a grand adventure, and the journey only continues from here.

"Don't try to figure it out. Just get really, really excited about it.
Be excited about this journey. Feel passion again.
Feel alive again. Feel limitless again."

— THE COUNCIL

You are here to live your grand adventure. You are here to live the most extraordinary existence of human life, whatever that means for you. You are here to expand the potentials and the possibilities that exist for all of humankind. You are here to fully awaken to the truth of who you are, to come into realization, to integrate every part of you, and then to live as the embodied, enlightened master that you are, that you are here to be.

Your presence in physical form on the planet, at this time, is so very important. And you are invited in every moment and in every opportunity and in everything that presents itself to you to elevate the consciousness, to go beyond, to expand what is possible, to see from a grander perspective, to bring a new awareness, to raise the vibration, to raise the frequency. Everything is your opportunity, dear master. Everything is your opportunity to alchemize all things back into the light so that it can be created and recreated in alignment to the highest good, to the Divine will, to the greater, grander picture of what is really going on here in your human experiences.

We understand in times like this you begin to take things seriously. There seems to be a lot going on in your world right now but remember that you are the conduit of Divine light in the world. You are the love in the world. You are the bringers of peace and harmony. You are here to embody your sovereignty and your freedom. You are here to be an example of well-being and abundance and possibility. You are here to shine your bright, beautiful light into every corner of this beautiful Earth experience.

A NEW EARTH REALITY

We have been talking for some time about a New Earth reality. A New Earth reality is birthed from a new level of consciousness, which summons new energy that allows the New Earth reality to begin to manifest in physical form. In every moment you are either birthing New Earth realities, or you are recreating the old. You are contributing to the separation and the lack and the limitation by denying and doubting your power and withholding love for yourself, questioning your infinite worth when we assure you that you and only you can keep you from being the bright, beautiful light of potential and possibility in this human experience.

Everything you feel, everything you think, your beliefs, the stories you tell yourself about yourself, and about your life, are creating your reality. You are here to live the most extraordinary life experience, which is why we say live boldly, dear master, shine brightly, dear master, play and create with all of creation, dance and sing and celebrate who you are and who you have become. You are realized masters, meant to come into the light, vibration, and frequency of the truth of who you are, to realize enlightenment while in physical form, and contribute to the raising of the consciousness and the raising of the vibration of your beloved human family.

These are extraordinary times, and you are an extraordinary being, and there are extraordinary potentials and possibilities here for you. You matter. Your life matters. You are in this time of the greatest transformation of human consciousness. We want you to understand how important that is. Every problem, every issue, everything that you see as a challenge or an unwanted reality is elevated, is expanded into new potentials as you raise your consciousness.

Consciousness is everything, which is why you drew this to you, which is why we say we are here, because we promised we would be so that you can never forget who you are. And as you elevate your consciousness, the illusion of limitation and lack and separation falls away. You begin to live fearlessly and follow energy fearlessly and follow the light fearlessly and pursue your dreams and desires and highest excitement with absolute freedom beyond any fear because you know who you are and the power within you and what is possible for you.

When you are presented with things that seem like challenges, difficulties, or complications, your first step is to come into the moment and into your power. We encourage taking three deep breaths, breathing in, breathing in again, and breathing in again to feel your power in the moment. And from there as you elevate your consciousness and you elevate your awareness and you allow yourself into a grander perspective of what's really going on here, all of a sudden that challenge or that difficulty or that problem or that complication seems so much smaller because you are so much clearer and more confident.

Always remember in every situation that there is a grander perspective, and if you are in lack or limitation or fear or separation, you are holding yourself apart from that grander perspective. In every moment, you have the opportunity to accept what is, and in the moment you accept what is, you let go of all resistance, and that is so important. The instant manifestation is peace, peace within you, peace around you. And in the moment you accept what is, the instant manifestation is peace.

THE HUMAN EXPERIENCE AS A GRAND ADVENTURE

The Council tells us that the most accurate description of why we are here and why we came to this human experience is for a *grand adventure*. You might be able to relate to this explanation by considering the example of going on a vacation. If you want to go on a vacation—let's imagine you want to plan the vacation of a lifetime. At this moment, you might be sitting in your warm, comfortable home with everything that you need, yet you feel *this call* to plan the adventure that you have always wanted to have—a journey you have always wanted to take, a vacation, a trip of a lifetime, or calling you have felt to a particular place.

In some cases, you might not know exactly why you have always felt called to a particular place, but it's piqued your interest. You may notice that you keep hearing about it, and you want to step away from your comfortable home and the things you wanted or needed, to have a new experience, to meet new people, to try new foods, to explore new cultures, to go to new places and see what it's like. And on this vacation, you might do activities you've never done before or spend time doing what you most enjoy, like reading, relaxing, dining out, or spending time in nature.

You plan your vacation and the details of the adventure you are about to have. Then, you board a flight or jump in your car and head out to your vacation destination. Once there, you have an incredible time, amazing experiences, and it's truly a grand adventure! You might be there for several days, weeks, or maybe even a month. But after a while, the time comes and you are ready to return home—it's time to *go home*. Why? Because it feels *so good* to be home. It feels so good to be home in *your* bed with *your* pillow, *your* blankets, *your* pets, *your* children, *your* friends, and *your* family—*it feels so good to be home.*

The Council tells us this is a wonderful analogy to explain why we came from nonphysical, Source Energy and focused ourselves into the human experience for this *grand adventure*. And once we've enjoyed this grand adventure and the adventure is complete, we *return home* to Source Energy. Why? Because, again, *it's so good to be home.* Until the next adventure calls us, and we move forth once again from that experience of being home—one with Source Energy—to have the next vacation, grand adventure, or vacation of a lifetime.

Life is meant to be good for you. It's meant to be joyful. You're meant to have fun. You're here for a grand adventure. All experiences that you have here on Earth provide data and information that bring you into new levels of clarity, wisdom, perspective, expansion, and existence.

It's all here for you. And you don't all choose the same adventures. Years ago, I read a book by Shirley MacLaine called *The Camino*, about the Camino de Santiago. I kept hearing about it. I had no idea what it was, but I kept seeing posts about it on social media and came across a movie about it. When I saw the book, I felt called to read it; I couldn't put it down. I read the entire book in one day. When I finished the book, I thought, "Someday I'm going to take a trip and I'm going to go walk the Camino!"

Over the years, I've had many friends who have walked the Camino and they've all had completely different experiences. Each time I hear someone's story, I think, "That's an adventure I'd like to have someday!" It is still an adventure I want to have, and I know someday it will happen.

I've had other experiences, like going to Bora Bora. Many years ago, I saw a movie and I could not get the scenes of the place where the movie was filmed out of my mind. It was the most beautiful place I had ever seen. I was determined to find out where the movie was filmed and go there. I discovered that it was filmed in Bora Bora near Tahiti in French Polynesia.

From the moment I watched the movie, I was obsessed and felt called to go to Bora Bora. I thought about it constantly, and one day my partner asked where I wanted to go on our next vacation. Immediately, I blurted out, "Bora Bora!" Before long, we began to plan our grand adventure, and the time came to pack and head to the airport.

Bora Bora was everything I imagined it to be—truly the most beautiful place in the world. I had an amazing vacation. It was indeed a grand adventure. I met incredible local people. I tasted delicious new foods and tried new activities.

One of the activities was a Jet Ski tour around the island of Bora Bora. At some point in the tour, one of the locals guided us to a beach where we stopped. He parked his Jet Ski, jumped off, and immediately climbed up in a palm tree to grab a couple of coconuts. He came down all excited to show us all the different benefits of a coconut. He explained that every part was useful. The outside of the coconut was used as a loofah to clean yourself or brush your teeth. The milk of the coconut could be used for sunscreen, and in fact, had for hundreds and thousands of years been used by the local people to protect themselves from the sun. The coconut water was filled with nutrients and thus was used for hydration, while the meat of the coconut was used as food for survival.

I never forgot that experience and often reflect on it when The Council shares how our human experiences are just like a vacation where we try new things, meet new people, and uncover new data and information. As you go on your own adventures, explore new people, have new experiences, try new things, it adds and expands all that you are. Not because you're not enough as you are, but because it expands you. Does knowing all that I learned about the coconut make me more worthy in the eyes of Source, God, the Divine, or my soul? Of course not! But it's fun, it's exciting, it's part of the grand adventure.

In addition to this grand adventure that you call your life experience, you are also on a journey. It is the journey of the soul, the journey from Oneness with Source to a unique expression of Source, and to then return to Source once again. To understand this journey and how it only continues from here, let's explore the different levels of consciousness that are part of our journey here on Earth.

LEVELS OF CONSCIOUSNESS

Let's begin with the 3rd Dimension, which is a dimension of consciousness here on Earth. This dimension of consciousness is characterized by separation, in which you experience being apart from or disconnected from all else. A common experience for many in the 3rd Dimension is to perceive things in polarities—good or bad, right or wrong. It's also common to think that you are just your body, and anything that is not your body is outside of you, separate from you, not part of you. It is also characterized by separation from Source, God, the Divine, Spirit, or your Soul.

You are one with Source. You focused yourself into your own unique expression. You came into this physical experience. You are separate from that nonphysical part of you most of the time, but especially when focused in the 3rd Dimension. You think you are your problems, issues, circumstances, and the bad things that happened to you. You are interrupting life through your physical senses such as what you see, hear, taste, touch, and smell.

The experience on this part of the journey though consciousness is that we are separate from other people. You're in *this body*. They're in *that body*. You're thinking your thoughts in your head. They're thinking their thoughts in their head. And you think you're separate. When you want something, you experience it as *out there*. A person might describe what they want and say, "It's out there and I'm here and I want that over there, but I'm separate from it, so I must go out and get it."

When you are in separation from what you think you want or need, and separate from others, and separate from Source, it leads to an experience of lack, limitation, fear, and struggle. When someone is in the 3rd Dimension of separation, they experience limitation, and they also impose limitation upon themselves and others.

The dimension you are in is determined by your vibration. The 3rd Dimension has a lower vibration and can be described as a dense, or often heavy, experience. It doesn't mean you can't achieve things or accomplish things, but in the 3rd Dimension, people believe they have to push, force, effort, work really hard, or take massive action over long periods of time to arrive at what it is they want. Not to mention, they often arrive at that result completely exhausted because of the density they incurred in the 3rd Dimension.

In the 3rd Dimension, a person might feel they are the labels they've been given, such as: parent, spouse, employee, boss, successful, good, etc. However, when something happens like the death of a loved one, the loss of a job, failure of a business, end of a relationship, or life-threatening disease, they might find themselves asking the question, "Who am I?"

This often occurs because people don't know who they are, for example, if they have been someone's wife for 30 years and now that marriage has ended. Or, they have worked so hard to become a manager at their job and now they have been laid off. Add to it the inability to pay their bills, which may then cause them to lose their home, business, or incur a large amount of debt.

This often leads to what is referred to as an *awakening experience.* One begins to realize that they are not their circumstances and conditions. They can change their circumstances and conditions. Simply asking the question, "Who Am I?" begins to raise one's vibration.

When someone awakens to the potential that they are more than their circumstances and conditions and discovers they can begin to change those circumstances and conditions, they begin to move into the 4th Dimension of transformation. In this dimension, you can change things, you can fix things, you can heal things, you can transmute things, you can release things, you can process things.

The 4th Dimension is a state of consciousness where one is in a higher vibration than the 3rd Dimension of separation. Many people spend decades or their entire adult lifetime in the 4th Dimension of transformation because they're always trying to fix or change something about themselves, like losing weight, looking younger, getting more fit, eating better, making more money, healing their body or their past stories, changing this and changing that.

When you are always looking at what needs to be fixed and changed about you and others, you are in judgment. To take the step from the 4th Dimension into the 5th Dimension of pure love, you must choose to let go of judgment of yourself, others, and circumstances and conditions. The 5th Dimension is characterized by the experience of pure love within yourself that creates a Heaven on Earth type state of consciousness.

In the 5th Dimension of pure love, your well-being and your abundance is assured. You feel a sense of peace, harmony, joy, fulfillment, inspiration, and connection. You are fully allowing Source Energy. You are coming into your mastery. You are coming into self-realization. You are creating your reality, but not from a place of *you're not enough* or there's something wrong with you, but aligned to your wholeness, completeness, and the perfection that is your true nature. Then you create more of what you are *because it's fun!*

The 6th Dimension is also part of our journey as a soul through the human experience. It is the realm of pure potential and possibility, or what some might refer to as *imagination.* It's a dimension of consciousness that you access here when in physical form. However, it's a formless dimension where we explore the many potentials and possibilities that exist in form and the feeling of those realities in form.

Imagine waking up in a beautiful little cottage located on the ocean. You can hear the waves crashing on the beach and the seagulls calling out to one another. It's a bright, sunny day, and you are going to go for a walk on the beach. Imagine walking on the beach and feeling the warm sand beneath your feet. You can feel the crisp, cool water as the waves roll onto the beach. The sunshine on your face feels as good as the gentle breeze in the air kissing your cheek. As you imagine all of this, notice that you are envisioning all these things in form. The 6th Dimension allows us to continue our journey into expansion, expression, and experiences that are limitless, but often still imagined in form.

These are the four essential dimensions that The Council refers to when they talk about the levels of consciousness available to each of us here in the human experience. However, the journey only continues from here. Someday, when you transition from this Earth plane, release the density of the body, and return to nonphysical, the journey will go on—you will go on as the eternal being that you are. You will continue your journey through even higher levels of consciousness that are available to you when you're no longer in physical form. And some of those dimensions might very well be dimensions of consciousness that are formless.

Not only where *you* are formless, but the dimensions of consciousness are formless. I don't know that our human brains are ever going to completely figure that out because of the way we're created to thrive in physical form here on Earth with bodies, brains, and physical senses.

When your journey continues and you release the density of the body, you are continuing on the soul's journey in higher levels of consciousness, but you will always exist. Consciousness is not limited to the brain or the body. And you really begin to understand that more as we explore what opens you up to experience the 5th Dimension of pure love later in this section.

EXISTENCE IS ETERNAL

In 2022, I had a very dear friend make his transition. I had the great privilege and blessing to be with him, his wife, and his daughters on the final day of his life. Although there were many tears knowing he would soon leave the body, my experience was that there was only love. Behind the tears and emotions we were feeling, there was this great love for this man that we all cared so much about. Behind all emotions, there is always an opportunity to connect back to the love. If one goes beyond the grief or sadness they might be feeling, you will arrive at the knowing that you feel this way because you love. You love a person, place, animal, etc.

After my friend passed, I received several beautiful messages from him using the process of automatic writing, as did his wife and some close friends. For the first two years, anytime I tuned in to him on the other side, I instantly received a message and awareness of his presence around me. One day, I went to tune in and I had a very clear, powerful knowing that he was now continuing his journey on in what felt like much higher levels of consciousness.

I knew his existence was eternal, and for the first time, I had an absolute knowing that he now continues on his journey in what felt like dimensions of consciousness far beyond the human experience, what felt like the 12th Dimension or higher. Some days later I mentioned to his wife that I had a sense that his journey had now taken him to much higher vibrations and levels of consciousness. She concurred and said she had the same feeling just days prior that he had moved far beyond. This was one of the best examples I've ever had of understanding that the journey only continues on from here.

The Council focuses their messages on the dimensions of consciousness that you access here in the physical experience and that which best supports you in creating your best life, a life you love, and being all that you are. However, becoming aware of your own journey, why you chose to come here, and that you are here on this grand adventure, can be very empowering and inspiring. Expanding your awareness also allows you to transcend the illusions that often occur in the human experience.

The ultimate illusion, misunderstanding of the human experience, and single thing that often causes the greatest amount of suffering on our planet is the belief in death. While death often feels very real when someone you love passes on, it is an illusion that could be better explained and understood. Everything is energy. Everyone is energy and consciousness. Energy and consciousness change form, but nothing ever dies.

No one ever dies. Life is a grand adventure if you will allow it to be. The journey only continues from here—for everyone. If you will remember this and apply this wisdom when someone that you love and care about is making their transition, your state of consciousness will elevate your vibration to allow the love that you are and the love of the person who has transitioned, even when they are no longer in form. In doing so, you alleviate your own suffering, and you make it possible to still connect to the consciousness and energy of your loved one.

This one is so powerful to me. I have applied it in my own life, and I have been able to allow those that I love—humans and animals—to make their transitions at the time of their choosing, without the grief that I used to experience. If you have a loved one who is near the time when they are about to transition or has recently transitioned, come back to this powerful principle to remember this truth.

Consciousness moves energy into form; this is the formula for all creation.

"Thriving is not about circumstances and conditions. It's about the amount of energy you're summoning into your experience. When someone is thriving, it's not because their circumstances and conditions are always all perfect. It may appear that way, and it may be that way, and it might feel that way, but what really created the experience of thriving was the expansion of consciousness and the summoning of energy that led to the enhanced circumstances and conditions or the expanded circumstances and conditions."

— THE COUNCIL

You are living in exciting times. You are here for the greatest transformation of human consciousness that has ever occurred, and you are either seeing something like a war or a pandemic or a crisis, or you are seeing consciousness in action, love in action, transformation, transcendence, and revelation.

Do not lose your way. Do not get discouraged. Do not fight against yourself or anyone; we assure you the battle is never *out there*. It is about consciousness in the moment and being present to a grander perspective, a higher awareness where anything and everything is possible for you and for all of humankind.

You can look around at current events and say, "Oh, that's terrible," no matter when you read this. You could always find something every day in your news, in your media to say, "Oh, that's awful, and that's terrible, and that shouldn't be happening. No, really this shouldn't. No, no, really, this really is bad. No, really this is awful. This really shouldn't be happening." You can justify and fight for your limitation and entangle and judge. And there is no judgment from our side ever, but you are either holding yourself in limitation and separation or you are embodying the master that you are, the wayshower that you are in this moment, and creating new pathways, new levels, new frontiers. You cannot do that if you're entangled or feeling victimized.

There will always be something that, if you want to look outside of you for why you cannot find happiness within you, there will always be something you could use—what's going on in the world or in your family—to argue why you cannot experience joy in this moment. And there is no judgment from our side ever, but that's how powerful you are. You are either perceiving Heaven on Earth or Hell. They're not out there in the afterlife. They're states of consciousness here and now. They are a way of perceiving reality. They are a state of consciousness determined by your vibration and your frequency.

The only thing that changes anything is energy. The only thing that changes the body, the only thing that allows for spontaneous healings, the only thing that creates transformation in the body and your relationships with your families, with your children, is the energy that flows forth into new forms of manifestation, and this energy can only change through consciousness.

The greatest transformational force on your planet is love. The most powerful force is love. It could also be explained as consciousness because as you elevate your consciousness and your awareness there is only love.

Consciousness and awareness and love are what create change and transformation, but you do not have to entangle with lack and limitation and separation to experience the expansion that occurs through the elevation of your consciousness and your awareness, because consciousness is what summons the energy for grand, glorious manifestations in physical form. Consciousness, the elevation of consciousness and awareness is what moves the energy needed into form to create change.

When you really understand this, you no longer react to the external world. You will never again experience fear. You will not worry about anything. You will not struggle, and you will not suffer. And if you want to positively contribute to humanity and create a path forward out of suffering, the answer is consciousness, the consciousness that results in an unwavering force of love. And it is that force of love that can do the impossible because of the level of consciousness that summons the energy for great change.

Consciousness is what moves energy into form. It's the formula for all of creation. You have this awareness. Now watch it create miracles in your life and in the lives of others.

THE FORMULA FOR ALL CREATION

Who wouldn't want to know the precise formula for all of creation? Well, here it is: consciousness moves energy into form. This is *the* formula for all creation. Your level of consciousness determines the level of energy you are summoning into form.

As you raise your vibration and your consciousness, you begin to access more energy than when you are in lower levels of consciousness. When you elevate your consciousness, you're also expanding or elevating your vibration and increasing your frequency, which creates a force field of consciousness that expands and now includes so much more than it did when you were in a lower vibration, a slower frequency, or in a lower level of consciousness.

I highlight this very important point: Being in a different level of consciousness or a lower level or a higher level is not a hierarchy. In the eyes of Source, God, the Divine, our souls, *we are all one* and we are all worthy. It is understood that we will experience different levels of consciousness at different times throughout our grand adventure.

There is never any judgment. These examples of consciousness are never intended to create some sort of hierarchy that those who are in a higher dimension of consciousness are *better than*. It is simply an opportunity to raise your consciousness to live your best life—to live your highest potential—with greater ease, joy, harmony, freedom, well-being, abundance, and freedom. It's about opening up to all that is here for you; that this truly was and is meant to be a grand adventure.

From a perspective of observation—without judgment—can you think of a person in your life who is stuck in the 3rd Dimension of separation living in fear, lack, and limitation? If you were to tell them life is meant to be a grand adventure, they might think you are crazy. If you told them life is like a vacation, they might quickly respond with how they are afraid to fly, don't have the money to go on a vacation, hate traveling, don't like new places or people. You still love them just the same even if they are holding themselves in lack, limitation, and fear.

Understanding and consciously choosing the level of consciousness you are in, doesn't make anyone better than anyone else. It certainly might make your life a whole lot better when you consciously choose to go beyond lack, limitation, fear, and judgment to experience pure love and create the life you want. We choose our experiences. And just like you choose your experiences, you choose your level of consciousness. This determines how expansive your force field of consciousness is in each moment, which determines the level of energy you are summoning, which determines your experiences in physical form. And *it's all your energy*. It is the energy of Source—you are Source Energy, you came from this Source Energy, this Source Energy is what you are.

As you raise your vibration and increase your frequency, you come into the highest levels of consciousness and instantly begin to summon more of your own Source Energy in this moment. That energy will take whatever form is in the highest and best good for you, most serves you, is most advantageous for you, and delivers to you in that moment everything you need and more. This Source Energy delivers to you the abundance and the well-being that is assured in the 5th Dimension of pure love.

The energy that you summon through your consciousness can take shape in many different forms. It might come in the form of an inspired idea. It might come in the form of an inspired action. It might come in the form of following the inspiration to go to the store, getting to the store to see it's closed, turning around, and seeing the sunshine and the blue sky over your house where everyone else is experiencing stormy, cloudy weather. It might take the form of an ability, money, new job, new relationship, book that you write, garden that you plant, business you start, or song that you sing. It can take all sorts of forms, and it will take the form that is in your highest and best good *in that moment.*

The form it takes might be a new creation or something that is already in form that moves into your reality. People often think, "Oh, so I'm summoning my energy into form through my consciousness to experience something moving out of thin air into my physical form." Sometimes it will happen that way. It also includes everything that is already in form. In summoning energy in the moment, that form then moves into your experience, or you are guided clearly through the summoning of energy to that form which already exists.

When you are raising your consciousness, you are summoning more energy. You are becoming a more expansive conduit of Source Energy. You are becoming a more expansive force field of consciousness. You are becoming more magnetic, more powerful, more radiant. You are becoming a more expansive *light* that is seen throughout the entire Universe and radiates, magnetizes, attracts *to you* everything you need and more.

CONSCIOUSNESS MOVES ENERGY INTO FORM

This is the success principle that will *guarantee* there is no reason for you to ever worry about anything ever again, because you know you can elevate your consciousness and summon your own Source Energy into form for everything you need and more in any moment. Why would you ever worry about what you are going to say or do or need or struggle with in the future, when you know that in each now moment you can become conscious and summon to you all that is available to you in that moment.

You might be worried about a big conversation that you have to have with someone. Maybe it's your boss, employee, family member, child, or spouse. You might be worried about what you are going to say, or what they are going to say, or creating a story in your head of the worst-case scenario. Worrying only, and always, slows your vibration, lowers your frequency, moves you into lack and limitation, and creates fear. Fear equals fewer options. When you think it's going to go this way or that way, it creates a sense of fear, which slows your vibration, lowers your consciousness, limits the flow of Source Energy, and diminishes the potentials and possibilities available to you in the moment.

However, if you know in every moment—which you do—you can always access the highest level of consciousness in any moment, then all you're focused on is your consciousness level in the moment because you know that being in a higher level of consciousness is summoning more energy into the form of the highest words, the highest outcome, the highest potential in this situation. It is the formula for all creation.

The same is true when starting a project, job, business, or venture. You don't know what resources you're going to need. You don't know what opportunities are going to come. You don't know every step along the way. This is also true of life—the grand adventure. You don't know how the vacation is going to unfold exactly. But, if you know consciousness moves energy into form and you know that that is the formula for all creation, in any moment you can focus on being in the highest level of consciousness, being in the highest level of awareness, having a grander perspective, and in that level of consciousness, you're summoning energy in that moment, becoming the most expansive conduit of Source Energy, becoming the most expansive force field, drawing to you everything you need and more. And everything will come, everything you need will be there.

Consciousness can also be referred to or thought of as *awareness*. Awareness draws to you everything you need and more. Your own awareness is what expands the potentials and the possibilities of the moment. Expanding your awareness allows you to see what others do not.

If you think about consciousness as awareness, having a bigger picture, having a grander viewpoint, expanding this conduit of light that shines upon all that is here for you, you can very easily see how that summons energy into form and why that is the formula for all creation. It might be helpful to think about consciousness as awareness.

A HIGHER VIBRATION IS YOUR NATURAL STATE OF BEING

The most common question people ask as it relates to this success principle is, "How do I elevate my consciousness and raise my vibration?" Being in a higher vibration and higher state of consciousness is your natural, inherent state of being. It's about becoming aware of when and how you lower your vibration and frequency.

Think about a time you were feeling deflated or defeated. Or maybe a time you felt worried or overwhelmed. Think about how you were feeling in your body when you were in that state. Your shoulders might be down, your head might be hanging down, your eyes might be looking down toward the ground. You might equate this to your vibration being down and your consciousness level lowered.

Now imagine that you start to feel better. You pick your head up and start to look around at what's in front of you. Now, suddenly, there's a lot more opportunity and potential than what you could see just on the ground as you were looking down. You start to see a higher viewpoint with your eyes toward the sky. There is so much more in front of you and available to you from this perspective.

As you raise your vibration, as you raise your frequency, you sit up a little taller now, a little straighter, you can see everything on the horizon in front of you. You begin to elevate your consciousness and awareness a little more and you realize you can see everything on both sides of you. Then you turn around to look behind you, you look above you, and you look all around you. Now, suddenly, there's a whole lot more available to you.

This example might help you to understand how consciousness, awareness, a grander perspective, moves energy into form, and how it allows you to experience more of the potentials and possibilities that are around you. Another very simple way is when you're lowering your vibration you are collapsing the conduit of Source Energy that is available to you. You are contracting as you lower your vibration and your frequency. You are expanding as you raise your consciousness and vibration and elevate your frequency, and there's more available to you. You can image the expansion as more water flowing through a hose when there are no kinks. However, if you kink the hose, you slow the flow and limit the amount of water that can flow through the hose. In this example, the water is energy. When you expand the conduit of that energy or water, there is so much more that can flow through. There's more that can flow through to *you*.

Remember, sometimes in the moment when you are summoning energy into form, it might already be there; you just couldn't see it because you were so overwhelmed, looking down at the ground, limiting your perspective of what is possible for you. But, if you would have just picked your head up, you would have seen the answer, the form, the idea, the inspiration—what you needed was right there the entire time.

And it might come in the form of an inspired action or an inspired idea, or it might come in the form of an awareness of something guiding you—energy is guiding you toward something, or you have this sudden *knowing*. In many examples, what you are creating is already in form, but now it's moving to you powerfully because you have expanded your own force field of consciousness and conduit of light, and you are drawing to you that which is already in form and available to you. It's possible that it has already been physically created by something or someone else, but now it becomes part of your experience because you've expanded your consciousness and summoned the energy for it to move into form—into form, into your experience. Other times, you are literally directing the particles of infinite creation into form.

As you align to a higher level of consciousness, your well-being and your abundance are assured.

"You are in pure love. That is a state of consciousness that we refer to as the 5th Dimension, where your well-being and your abundance is assured, where what you want and need comes to you even before you know you need it, where things just show up and it's a yes, where there's this magical unfolding, where you do what you love and what brings you joy, where you follow the energy and let the light guide the way, where the next perfect step comes to you, where life surprises and delights you and excites you, and you play and create and dance with all of creation because it's all here for you.
You're already there. You're already experiencing it.
It's already your reality. How beautiful is that?"

— THE COUNCIL

Congratulations! *You made it!* You are ready to explore Success Principle Number 15.

As you align to a higher level of consciousness, your well-being and your abundance is assured. And this expands perfectly on what we were just talking about in Success Principle Number 14. You are summoning energy into form for your well-being and for your abundance. As you align to a higher level of consciousness, your well-being and abundance is assured.

This reminds me of one of my favorite teachings of The Council, one that changed my life at a time when I had some uncertainty specifically about bringing The Council's message to the world and how that would unfold. I had left my corporate career and everything that was safe and secure for me at that time. This meant I had no income and was living on my savings that were quickly dwindling.

I was channeling The Council and seeking an answer to my direction and financial situation. They said one of the most powerful affirmations for abundance was to say out loud and repeat, "Galore, galore, I have everything I need and more. Galore, galore, I have everything I need and more. Galore, galore, I have everything I need and more."

The first time I recited the affirmation, the immediate thought in my head said, "No, I don't have everything I need. I need more or I am going to run out soon. I need more of this; I need more of that." The second time the thought in my head was, "Okay, well, yeah, *technically*, in this moment, I have everything I need, technically, I guess." By the third time I repeated the affirmation out loud, I started to realize I did have everything I needed in that moment. I kept affirming it day after day. I soon had the realization that all throughout my life, I may not have had everything I thought I wanted at that moment, but I did have everything I needed, and more.

I kept affirming it day after day and felt more and more empowered. And I kept affirming it and I began moving myself into the awareness of the truth of this statement. My mind settled and I started to believe it. Before long, all sorts of things started showing up, things started showing up right before I needed them. Money started showing up in unusual ways, and if an unexpected expense occurred, I had the money and more to pay for it.

It started to expand beyond a concept of abundance into realizing I have all the resources I need and more. I have all the wisdom I need and more. I have all the time I need and more. I have all the connections I need and more. I have all the love I need and more. And it just kept expanding and expanding.

FIRST AWARENESS, THEN ABUNDANCE

The Council tells us that first comes the awareness. Oftentimes, when you first hear something like "Galore, galore, I have everything I need and more," you might notice that your current beliefs are directly opposed to what you are becoming aware of. That's fine. In fact, it's quite normal. Just allow yourself to continue to perceive it.

I became aware of this truth that "galore, galore, I have everything I need and more," and I started to perceive it as possible, and then I started to experience it. It started to show up in my reality. And as it did, it became truth to me. As it became the truth of my reality, it continued to expand, and more and more kept showing up for me. Not only can I now say, "galore, galore, I have everything I need and more," my truth is that "galore, galore, I have everything I want and more, galore, galore, I want everything I have and more," and I have come to the place of absolute knowing that my well-being and abundance is assured. If this was possible for me in my situation with no job, no income, and no certainty of my direction forward, I assure you it is possible for you too.

This is one of the powerful realizations of coming into the 5th Dimension of pure love. In the 5th Dimension of pure love, your well-being and your abundance is assured. What you want and need shows up before you know you need it. When you remember that you get more of what you are and, instead of wanting something from a place of lack, you affirm, "I love the abundance in my life. I love the freedom in my life. I love the connections in my life," and you begin to focus on all that you have, you will find meaning in the abundance you have, in the connections you have, and it expands. It could be no other way. It expands; you get more of what *you are.*

I want to share another comment from this course. My student told me, "I want to share my experience using The Council's wisdom to overcome a health issue. I was exercising two months ago when I had an abdominal cramp. It was very painful. I practiced breathing three times, taking three deep breaths, then going down to my heart and feeling love radiating from my heart to my belly. I started thinking and affirming, 'I love you, I love you, I love you.' I visualized my love radiating out, embracing my abs. About two minutes later, I could feel my three muscles relax one by one by one, and I no longer felt any pain after that. My well-being was assured!"

This is such a beautiful example of how in the moment someone was experiencing pain, that instead of going into fear, overwhelm, or resistance, this person went into a higher level of consciousness. She went into the level of consciousness that summoned the energy to relax the tension in her body and experience her well-being. She went to a place of love. She took three deep breaths. She went from her head into her heart. She focused on love for her body. She visualized love radiating through her body. And she allowed the energy to move the experience of well-being into form.

This same process works for anything and anyone, *truly*. It works for anything. This is also a wonderful example of how you can raise your consciousness. I want to make this point clear and consumable because many people ask the questions, "How do I raise my consciousness? How do I raise my vibration? How do I raise my frequency?"

Being in a state of pure love is your natural, innate, inherent state of being. You have learned how to lower your consciousness. You have learned how to move yourself into lower levels of consciousness. You have learned how to lower your vibration and slow down your frequency. Here's an example that many people can relate to in their lives. Think about how you or others have learned to respond to something that happens by saying, "Oh, that's awful. Oh, that's terrible." This is a response that many people have learned from others, and they unconsciously repeat when something comes up and a person immediately goes into unconscious judgment about it.

The Council says that we only have two innate human fears: the fear of falling and the fear of loud noises. If you're around a baby and you walk up behind them and make a loud noise, they get startled and they will likely cry, it's the fear of loud noises. If you watch a baby when they first learn to walk and they fall, they likely will cry, the fear of falling. All other fears are learned.

Everything else that you fear, you have learned throughout your life experience. The 5th Dimension of consciousness, that vibration, that higher frequency, that state of pure love, is your innate, inherent, natural state of being. Instead of worrying about how to raise your vibration, raise your frequency, it might be easier to consciously, lovingly observe the ways that you lower your vibration, your consciousness, and your frequency.

HOW YOU LOWER YOUR VIBRATION AND HOW TO RAISE IT

Here are some common, unconscious, habitual ways of thinking that lower one's vibration and consciousness level: I'm not good enough. Nothing I do is ever good enough. I always must do everything on my own. I've never been smart. I've never been good at this or that. I am not thin enough, young enough, tall enough. I am alone and have no support. I don't know what I am supposed to do. I don't know how. Nothing ever works out for me.

Most people are completely unaware of their own unconscious, habitual ways of thinking that lower their consciousness and vibration. These statements are unconscious habits that are often passed down and learned in childhood, in the education system, from people you are associated with as you go through your life. It's not a conspiracy, truly. Unknowingly, we are often taught to go against our natural state of being.

This awareness is your opportunity not to push against or blame yourself or others for the things that lower your vibration or consciousness. It's your opportunity to realize that you can return to your natural state of being in a consciousness and vibration of pure love. That's why you have drawn all this to you. That's why you have awakened. That's why you are on this journey of coming into realization—to live your highest potential, to be self-realized, to integrate every part of you into your wholeness, into your completeness, into your perfection, and live fully, love fully, and be all that you are. That is why you're *here*!

Once you understand this, you could quite easily make a list of all the ways that we lower our vibration. Stress, worry, overwhelm, unconscious thoughts, believing that we're not good enough, believing we're not smart enough, pushing against what is, getting distracted, judging ourselves, and many other examples we have talked about. Don't judge it. Just be conscious of when you're unconsciously holding yourself in limitation. Be conscious of when you're unconsciously lowering your vibration or your consciousness. Be aware and remember that your natural inherent state of being is pure love.

One of the easiest ways to quickly raise your vibration is to ask one simple question: "What brings me joy?" And start focusing on the things that bring you joy. Start imagining that you are doing the thing that brings you joy. Go do the things that bring you joy as often as possible all throughout your day. Instantly, you will raise your vibration when focused on *joy*.

If I were to ask myself the question, the answer might be my dog, my cats, my horses, my partner, nature, sunsets, birds, animals of all kinds, roses, flowers, the ocean, music, baths, candles. I could go on and on and on. As I focus on the things that bring me joy, like nature, I can feel the sensation of the sunshine on my face. You can literally feel your vibration rising. You can feel in your body that your consciousness is being elevated, and suddenly, now you're summoning a whole lot more energy.

You will know the difference between whether you're in a higher level of consciousness or lower. When you notice you're in a lower level of consciousness, if you feel that your vibration isn't where you want it to be, the most important thing is not to judge yourself for that. Love yourself. Stop and take some deep breaths, go from your head into your heart, and ask the question, "What brings me joy?"

When you focus on joy, you will naturally feel your way into the 5th Dimension of pure love. A common question then becomes, "How do we live in a state of pure love?" Remember, pure love *is* your natural state of being. Do not deny love for yourself and don't doubt that you are worthy of the love that you are and the love that you feel. Be aware in the moment and observe, are you in some way denying love for yourself? It might be through the thoughts you are thinking about yourself, or an old story, or an old belief in your head. It might sound like this: "I don't have the money to do what I want. It's so hard to meet someone. I need to lose this weight. I have never been very smart. I am the worst when it comes to spelling. If I don't do *this thing*, people won't like me. Nobody cares about me."

These are ways one denies love for oneself. Instead, move into your wholeness, your perfection, your completeness, exactly as you are right now. Notice if you're denying love for yourself with a story that you're telling, or an old belief that you have, or an unconscious or habitual way of thinking.

A common way this shows up for a lot for people is denying themselves the time, or the opportunity, or the experience of *doing* the things they love and enjoy. I can think of a particular person in my life who loves skiing, absolutely loves skiing—always talking about how much they love to ski. However, this person hasn't skied in many years because they believe they must work, make more money, can't ask for time off, can't spend the money to go do the thing they really love to do. This is an example of a way that one denies love for oneself.

This is different than being responsible. Of course, if you are always blowing off work to go ski and blowing all the money you have on ski trips, one might regard that as irresponsible. It's not about never showing up to work, blowing off your job all the time, and saying, "Oh, I'm just doing what I love all day."

However, as you apply this principle and become aware of allowing yourself to do the things you love, you might arrive at a place and time where you do create a life where you're doing what you love each day. Through consciousness, vibration, intention, joy and being in a state of pure love, you create the life where you *have* the freedom, abundance, and well-being to do what you love and enjoy each day.

CONNECT TO JOY AND PURE LOVE

One of my students asked the question, "When we are encouraged to focus on what brings us joy and follow the energy and the light, does that mean on days we don't feel guided to go to work or clean or cook or do grocery shopping, we should avoid those things? And we should change our plans last-minute if it feels forced or wrong to do them?"

The first thing I would suggest is to create time for yourself before you begin your day to connect to your joy, to your heart, to come into your power, to come into pure love. Intentionally, come into a state of pure love and raise your consciousness before you start your day.

I like to do this before I even open my eyes. When I wake up, I take three deep breaths. I go from my head into my heart. I like to focus and feel how blessed I am, how loved I am, how grateful I am for my life, and then, how excited I am for this day. I think about the things that bring me joy. I think about what I love. And then, I open my eyes. When I do this consistently, I notice that I have the most amazing day. If you don't have the opportunity right as you wake up, find some time throughout your day to reflect on these things and feel yourself move into a state of pure love through this exercise.

Consider for a moment *why* you do the things that you do each day or think that you must do each day. Why do you clean your house, cook, grocery shop, pay the bills? Why do you work? You might say, "I work because I like having the money I make at my job to do what I want to do when I want to do it. I work because I like having the money to pay my bills." As it relates to the question my student asked, before you decide that you do not want to go to work or question whether you should not go, avoid it, change plans, not do it, or not show up for something, first align to *why* you do a particular task or job, like cleaning, cooking, grocery shopping, or laundry.

If I think about my *perfect day,* it includes doing the work I love, playing with my horses, dog, and cats, and then cooking a delicious meal with my partner. I love sitting together in the evenings over dinner and talking about life, the adventures in our day, and eating a delicious meal together. However, that usually includes grocery shopping, cooking, cleaning. As I do those things, I remember how much I love and enjoy our precious time together over a delicious meal.

Sure, there are days I might feel like I don't want to cook and clean that day. However, if I take a moment and consider that one of the things I enjoy most in my *perfect day* is having a delicious meal with my partner, then I either summon the energy to joyfully do those things and head to the grocery store, or it's really clear to me on that day that I would prefer to do takeout, go out, or find other options.

The same thing is true when going to work. Take a moment to reconnect with why you do what you do. Be conscious, intentional, and focused on the meaning you're giving things. Why *are* you working? What *do* you enjoy about it? What *are* the blessings that come from your work? What *are* the gifts you receive from it? And then, it is your choice. You have the freedom to choose whether you're going to go to work. You have the freedom to choose whether you're going to quit your job. You have the freedom to do a whole lot of things. *But* the most important thing is your level of consciousness and state of being.

Come back to the awareness of your consciousness and vibration. Come back to the now moment and your presence. Come back into your power. Reconnect to a higher perspective and then let the energy and the light guide the way forward.

Another student asked, "Is it worth having desires, plans, goals, or should we just stay as happy as possible in the moment and allow things to show up?" This question was timely, as a dear friend of mine had recently suggested that on my birthday, which I was about to celebrate, that I do some inspired writing about what I wanted to experience in this new year.

I sat down in a quiet place, closed my eyes, took some deep breaths, and went into my imagination. I started to think about all the experiences that would be so fun to have this year. I thought about what I would most enjoy doing. I thought about what I would really love to do. Instead of writing a goal or making any plans, I thought to myself, "It would be so fun to experience *these things* this year," and then I started to write. I found that what flowed through me was very easy and felt uplifting.

Instead of setting goals per se, focus on what experiences would be fun to have. Ask yourself, "What would I love to experience? What am I excited about? What am I passionate about?" Write those things down. Go into your imagination and play with those potentials and possibilities. Then allow things to start showing up for you!

Within two hours of making that list of experiences that would be fun for me, I received a phone call *out of the blue* with an opportunity to do the exact thing that was on the top of my list. The exercise raised my vibration and level of consciousness, which assured my abundance and the summoning of my excitement into form.

TRUST YOUR INSPIRED IDEAS

This next example correlates to so many of the principles that we have discussed here. It highlights not having an agenda or being attached to an agenda, as *True Creation has no agenda.* It goes along with creating your reality, the meaning you're giving things, and everything that's happening for you. This very book you are reading is an example of all these things and how raising your level of consciousness beyond limitation assures your abundance and well-being.

When I was delivering the live course, The 15 Success Principles for Self-Realization, I was under contract with my publisher, Hay House, for my next book, which was due within a couple weeks. I love writing and working with my publisher. However, something just wasn't flowing, and I found my vibration lessening each time I sat down to work on the book.

I was one of those students in school who was taught that I needed to be a straight-A student. I had a programed belief that to be good enough or to be approved of I had to get straight A's. That meant that to do so you must follow a particular structure by which you meet your deadlines, you turn in your papers on time, you do your assignments on time. I could see that unconscious belief arise as I observed the lowering of my consciousness and vibration each time I went to work on the book.

As I sat down to work on the book, all I could feel was resistance. I would then go off and do something else, coming back to the book later only to feel the same resistance again. Reflecting on the success principles, I focused on coming into that stillness, feeling my way into the highest level of consciousness, and started feeling that I was no longer in resistance and now summoning energy. Instantly, an inspired idea came into form. What if I took this course and put it into a book, and I submitted *that* to my publisher instead of the book I was writing now?

I could feel the expansion. I could feel the excitement. I could feel the energy in that idea. And then my programming kicked in and my mind said, "But you're a straight-A student. You turn your things in on time. Now you're going to ask for more time and you're going to completely change the plan? That's crazy. It will never work."

Well, as you hold this book in your hands, it is the proof that consciousness moves energy into form. It is the proof that aligning to a higher level of consciousness will assure your well-being and abundance. And it is the proof that life truly is a grand adventure.

In this example, I was presented with the opportunity to apply several of those success principles to navigate through it with ease and arrive at the highest outcome. I would encourage you to observe the success principles in action in your own life! Reflect on your journey and how things have played out and how the amazing things that have been created in your life are a result of living and applying these success principles.

Channeled Activation for Experiencing Your True Self

We are so pleased and delighted to have the opportunity to speak with you on this fine and glorious day indeed. We remind you that while our words to you are important, this is a vibrational experience of the power within you, the love within you, the capacity within you to realize the highest expression of your soul in physical form.

You have the power to realize your perfection. You are everything you wish to be. You already are whole, complete, divine, infinite, eternal. You are infinitely worthy. Your capacity to allow your infinite worth will deliver to you the most rich, meaningful, purposeful experience of life and existence.

You cannot imagine how far you have come, and you truly will never figure out exactly where all of this is going. Enjoy the grand adventure. Take time to integrate all that you are. It may be a single breath to feel your Oneness. It may be the joyous experience of breathing in the life force that is here for you as you move through your experience on a daily basis with more joy, more love, more ease, more harmony, more freedom.

You are free. The integration of every part of you into your wholeness, completeness, and perfection has set you free. Stepping into your power has set you free. Coming into pure love has set you free, free to be all that you are, to create your reality, to choose the experiences that would be fun for you, dear master, because this is a grand adventure.

This is the journey you have chosen. You are exactly where you intended to be. And it will continue to get better and better and better as you allow yourself into more and more and more of all that you are, and you watch the potentials and the possibilities continue to expand as you realize more love, more joy, more passion, more freedom, more well-being, more abundance, more prosperity, more beauty, more meaning, more and more and more of the truth of who you are.

We are always with you. We are always available to you. You are us. We are you. You are The Council here on Earth. In every moment, know how loved you are, know how worthy you are, know how guided you are, know how supported you are in every moment. We are always with you. We are you.

We love you, we love you, we love you. And with that, we are complete.

Review: Expressing Your True Self

SUCCESS PRINCIPLE #13: Life is a grand adventure, and the journey only continues from here.

- Why go on a vacation, grand adventure, or trip of a lifetime? To meet new people, go new places, have new experiences, try new things.

- All experiences provide data and information that contribute to expansion.

- You continue the journey of the soul in higher levels of consciousness and new dimensions of existence.

SUCCESS PRINCIPLE #14: Consciousness moves energy into form; this is the formula for all creation.

- You are a force field of consciousness that is either expanded or contracted. This determines the level of energy you are summoning into form.

- Creation might take the form of inspired action, an inspired idea, a channeled message, manifestation of new form, or drawing to you something that is already in form.

SUCCESS PRINCIPLE #15: As you align to a higher level of consciousness, your well-being and your abundance is assured.

- Levels of consciousness in our human experience include: 3rd Dimension of Separation, 4th Dimension of Transformation, 5th Dimension of Pure Love, and 6th Dimension of Pure Potential.

- "Galore, galore, I have everything I need and more!"

- Pure Love is your natural state of being. Be aware of what lowers your consciousness and slows your vibration.

CONCLUSION

"Dear master, you have drawn this all to you. You have drawn this all to you. You have awakened just as you knew you would. You have come fully into realization just as you knew you would. And now you will realize the grandest vision and highest expression of all that you are in physical form just like you knew you would. You will know that you are the powerful Creator of your reality just as you knew you would. And you living your highest expression, your grandest vision, and the realization of the grand manifestations will inspire humanity, will inspire potentials and possibilities for all of humanity just as you knew it would."

— THE COUNCIL

These are the success principles for self-realization. Self-realization can often be explained as the feeling of pure love and a sense of Oneness. In the moment when you feel pure love and you feel Oneness within every cell of your body, you are integrating and allowing every part of you and coming into the knowing of your wholeness, your completeness, your perfection, your magnificence. You'll look back at everything that led you to that moment. I predict it will only expand your capacity to love, to experience the magic, miracles, manifestations, and the beautiful True Creation that's always presenting itself to you.

Self-realization just might be our highest potential of all in this life experience. It's the doorway to absolutely living the life of your dreams, creating your best life, being your best self. Not because you weren't enough or worthy before, but now you can express all that you already are—your highest Self. I truly think that is one of life's greatest gifts.

You have summoned to you not just how to move into the awareness of self-realization and the ability to start perceiving self-realization in your experience, but to actually *feel it*, to know it, to experience it as your reality. Then watch and enjoy the fun, the love, the way that life begins to present itself to you in the most miraculous way. You will know without question that through your alignment to a higher consciousness, your well-being and abundance is assured.

Once you openly allow the abundance and well-being that is assured to you, you can fully enjoy this grand adventure and everything you intended it to be. Witness all the ways that things show up even before you know you need them. That is my favorite part! Love yourself, express yourself fully, and know that you are everything you wish to be, *you already are.*

APPENDIX

The 15 Success Principles for Self-Realization

1. You are everything you wish to be. You already are.

2. You are Source Energy that you focused into a physical body.

3. You are the Creator within your own creation of reality.

4. What you focus on, and the meaning you give it, is what creates your reality.

5. Everything is always happening for you, not to you.

6. If you want to experience anything in the world around you, you must first create it within yourself.

7. You get more of what you are, not what you want.

8. When you are resisting anything, you are resisting everything.

9. All of your power is in the now moment.

10. There is no need to make a big decision about anything; allow all things to be choiceless.

11. True Creation has no agenda.

12. Stillness is the access point to acceleration.

13. Life is a grand adventure, and the journey only continues on from here.

14. Consciousness moves energy into form; this is the formula for all creation.

15. As you align to a higher level of consciousness, your well-being and abundance are assured.

ABOUT THE AUTHOR

Sara Landon is a globally celebrated author, speaker, transformational leader, spiritual teacher, and channel of The Council. She has been called the leader of leaders for the next generation of teachers, wayshowers, channels, coaches, and guides who are contributing to raising the consciousness and vibration on the planet at this time. Sara is the best-selling author of three books: *The Wisdom of The Council: Channeled Messages for Living Your Purpose; The Dream, The Journey, Eternity, and God: Channeled Answers to Life's Deepest Questions,* co-authored with *New York Times* best-selling author Mike Dooley; and *You Are a Channel: Receive Guidance from Higher Realms, Ascended Masters, Star Families, and More.*

As the voice of The Council, Sara's intention is to be the purest channel of their wisdom and teachings, which offer a grander perspective of what is possible for each of us—and our beloved human family—as we elevate our consciousness to new levels. She focuses herself, as the ultimate student, to live the wisdom and teachings at the highest level and is dedicated to helping others discover that they, too, have the ability to connect to these greater levels of awareness and guidance. Unique in the field of channeling, Sara not only shares The Council's wisdom but offers revolutionary guidance through personal practice on how to apply and integrate these teachings in everyday life for more joy, peace, ease, love, freedom, beauty, and abundance.

A powerful luminary, Sara's greatest joy is helping those who are ready to play in new levels of energy to reconnect with *all that they are,* so they may live, love, and lead in this time of awakening. Sara holds the vision of a fully awakened world, where all beings co-exist harmoniously with one another and Earth. Through numerous courses, coaching groups, and activations as well as her widely celebrated Global Masters Class program, she has helped thousands of people from around the world integrate the wisdom of The Council and create profound life-changing, long-lasting realization.

For more information and resources, please visit:
www.saralandon.com.

Hay House Titles of Related Interest

YOU CAN HEAL YOUR LIFE, the movie,
starring Louise Hay & Friends
(available as an online streaming video)
www.hayhouse.co.uk/louise-movie

THE SHIFT, the movie,
starring Dr. Wayne W. Dyer
(available as an online streaming video)
www.hayhouse.co.uk/the-shift-movie

*THE GOLDEN FUTURE: What to Expect and How to
Reach the Fifth Dimension,* by Diana Cooper

*THE AMAZING POWER OF DELIBERATE INTENT:
Living the Art of Allowing,* by Esther and Jerry Hicks

*THE AWAKENED WAY: Making the Shift to a
Divinely Guided Life,* by Suzanne Giesemann

*PLAYING THE MATRIX: A Program for Living Deliberately
and Creating Consciously,* by Mike Dooley

All of the above are available at your local bookstore,
or may be ordered by contacting Hay House (see next page).

We hope you enjoyed this Hay House book. If you'd like to receive our online catalogue featuring additional information on Hay House books and products, please contact:

Hay House UK Ltd
1st Floor, Crawford Corner,
91–93 Baker Street, London W1U 6QQ
Tel: +44 (0)20 3927 7290; www.hayhouse.co.uk

———

Published in the United States of America by:
Hay House LLC
PO Box 5100, Carlsbad, CA 92018-5100
Tel: (760) 431-7695 or (800) 654-5126
www.hayhouse.com

Published in Australia by:
Hay House Australia Publishing Pty Ltd
18/36 Ralph St., Alexandria NSW 2015
Tel: +61 (02) 9669 4299
www.hayhouse.com.au

Published in India by:
Hay House Publishers (India) Pvt Ltd
Muskaan Complex, Plot No. 3,
B-2, Vasant Kunj, New Delhi 110 070
Tel: +91 11 41761620
www.hayhouse.co.in

———

Let Your Soul Grow

Experience life-changing transformation – one video
at a time – with guidance from the world's leading experts.

www.healyourlifeplus.com

CONNECT WITH
HAY HOUSE
ONLINE

🌐 hayhouse.co.uk   f @hayhouse

📷 @hayhouseuk   🦋 @hayhouseuk.bsky.social

♪ @hayhouseuk   ▶ @HayHousePresents

'*The gateways to wisdom and knowledge are always open.*'

Louise Hay